MW01279960

MENTORING MADE
REAL

The Power of
Authentic Connection

NANCY LINDGREN

Founder
MORE Mentoring

Nancy is the real deal. She has a servant heart and is intentional about coming alongside others to love and empower them to be all that God has designed them to be. Her desire is to always see others enjoying a closer, more personal relationship with their Heavenly Father through the Word and prayer. I love our times together of authentic connection with prayer as the foundation of our mentoring relationship.

FERN NICHOLS
Founder of Moms in Prayer International
Author of *Moms in Prayer, Mom's Little Book of Powerful Prayers, When Moms Pray Together,* and *Igniting a Passion to Pray*
momsinprayer.org

You know a book is impactful when it prompts you to action. Nancy Lindgren's powerful and persuasive book on prayer-focused mentoring did just that. Her clarion call to reach out and come alongside another woman is delivered gently with words of kindness and simplicity. I read it to review it and ended up emailing a young mother God put on my heart and offering to mentor her. We start in just a few weeks. Instead of fretting over the amount of sadness and loneliness in this world, Nancy helps us do something and teaches us how with examples and encouragement. I highly recommend this book to all who are interested in helping another human being move closer to the God who loves them. I suspect all of us who answer Nancy's call will be forever changed in the best possible ways.

SHARON GAMBLE
Founder and Director of *Sweet Selah Ministries*
Author of *Sweet Selah Moments* and *Give Me Wings to Soar*
sweetselah.org

I have only had the privilege of knowing Nancy for several months, but I can say that in that short time her passion for Jesus, her passion for mentoring, and her passion to see people walk in the fullness for which they were created have inspired me. I am part of a team of ladies using her mentoring guide together, preparing our hearts to lead women one-on-one in our small mountain town start-up church. My prayer is that God will use this book to encourage you to see your potential in starting a ripple effect for the Kingdom of God—you walking alongside another person until she is rooted and grounded in Christ, and then the two of you doing the same for two more, and then the four of you doing the same for four more, etc. I'm eternally grateful that God has crossed my path with Nancy's.

SANDY BENSON
Founding team member of Alma Stone Church, Alma, CO

I sat down to read a couple of chapters of Nancy Lindgren's book, "Mentoring Made Real," and before I knew it, I was on Chapter 10. Whether a woman is considering becoming a mentor for the first time or is a well-seasoned mentor, Nancy's encouraging words are transparent and relatable. I had a sense of "I can do this" in the simplicity of the three words: Come. Be. Move. This book is filled with stories of authentic mentoring relationships and practical scriptural insights that give me great hope that "one-on-one, prayer-focused mentoring can change the world." This is a book I can't wait to get into the hands of our mentoring teams at our church.

DEBI LYDIC
Director of Women's Ministry
Valley Church, West Des Moines, IA

"Be available to Kim." Those are the words Nancy felt impressed on her heart by God. She reached out to ask if she could be my mentor and I was overjoyed! Nancy is emboldened with the Spirit and walks out in faithful obedience. When she asked about my expectations, I said, "I just want real." A relationship that is authentic. And that is what this book is all about: "Mentoring Made Real." She hears from the Lord. And this book is a product of her wisdom from experience and obedience in that. I'm grateful beyond words to be journeying life with her. You'll feel equally empowered to do the same after reading this book.

KIM CHURNESS
Mentee

When Nancy writes about authentic relationships and prayer-focused mentoring, it reminds me of the many prayer experiences I've had with her—including crawling under a stage to pray for an evangelist as he preached the gospel to a millennial crowd! Younger generations have always been on her heart. Nancy takes the complications and fear out of mentoring by focusing on the powerful simplicity of prayer. As she writes, Nancy shares her life, but she also shares her hope in Jesus. And that's what every woman needs!

CAROL MADISON
Author of *Prayer That's Caught and Taught: Mentoring the Next Generation*
Editor of *Prayer Connect* magazine

Someone has said, "A message prepared in a mind reaches minds; a message prepared in a heart reaches hearts; but a message prepared in a life reaches and changes lives." Nancy's life message of mentoring is expressed loud and clear in this book! I found myself wanting to find a mentor and a mentee for myself and apply all she shared. She makes it simple and attainable with the Lord's help. I'd encourage every woman to read this book and find someone to mentor!

ANGELA TEMPLES
Ambassador Program Director
Revive Our Hearts

Copyright © 2022 by Nancy Lindgren. All rights reserved.

ISBN: 979-8-986-5529-1-0

All Scripture quotations, unless otherwise indicated, are taken from the Holy Bible, New International Version®, NIV®. Copyright ©1973, 1978, 1984, 2011 by Biblica, Inc.™ Used by permission of Zondervan. All rights reserved worldwide. www.zondervan.com.

The "NIV" and "New International Version" are trademarks registered in the United States Patent and Trademark Office by Biblica, Inc.™

Scripture quotations marked "AMP" are taken from the Amplified® Bible, Copyright © 1954, 1958, 1962, 1964, 1965, 1987 by The Lockman Foundation. Used by permission.

Scripture quotations marked ESV are taken from the ESV® Bible (The Holy Bible, English Standard Version®), copyright © 2001 by Crossway, a publishing ministry of Good News Publishers. Used by permission. All rights reserved.

Scripture quotations marked "MSG" or "The Message" are taken from The Message. Copyright 1993, 1994, 1995, 1996, 2000, 2001, 2002. Used by permission. All rights reserved.

Scriptures taken from the Holy Bible, New International Reader's Version®, NIrV® Copyright © 1995, 1996, 1998, 2014 by Biblica, Inc. ™ Used by permission of Zondervan. www.zondervan.com. The "NIrV" and "New International Reader's Version" are trademarks registered in the United States Patent and Trademark Office by Biblica, Inc. ™

Cover photo by Elina Sazonova.

OTHER BOOKS

By Nancy Lindgren

TOGETHER: Come. Be. Move. - A mentoring guide for mentors & mentees
Book 1

TOGETHER: Come. Be. Move. - A mentoring guide for mentors & mentees
Book 2
(with Hannah Pipp)

TOGETHER: Come. Be. Move. - A mentoring guide for mentors & mentees
Book 3
(with Hannah Pipp)

TOGETHER: Going Deeper - A mentoring guide for mentors & mentees
Book 1
(with Merry Jo Orr)

TOGETHER: Walk With Me - A teen mentoring guide for mentors &
mentees
Book 1
(with Jeannine Mitchell)

TOGETHER: Guys Walking with the Wise - A men's mentoring guide for
mentors & mentees
Book 1
(with Mark Lindgren)

TOGETHER: First Steps - A mentoring guide for mentors & mentees
Book 1
(with Hannah Pipp)

JUNTAS: Venir. Estar. Movernos. - Una guia de mentoría para mentoras y
mentoreadas
Books 1, 2, 3 - Spanish translation
(with Hannah Pipp)

Thank you for purchasing *Mentoring Made Real*!

All of the author's proceeds from this book will help

support the ministry of MORE Mentoring.

morementoring.org

TABLE OF CONTENTS

INTRODUCTION

Seen. Heard. Known.

I want to be real with you. My life has had so many twists and turns and my journey hasn't always looked the way I thought it might. There have been long seasons of waiting, expectations that haven't been met, and longings unfulfilled. But I also have experienced fullness of life in ways I couldn't have dreamed up.

About two years ago, in the middle of a lot of unsettledness in our world, my husband and I decided to make a move to a small community in the mountains of Colorado—a place that's known for being "North America's HIGHEST Incorporated Town" at an elevation of 10,578 feet. I'm choosing to say we live the closest to heaven.

I know God brought us here for a reason. I just haven't fully known the reason quite yet. While enjoying the beautiful scenery and peacefulness of being away from a big city, that first year I was lonely.

We were "going to church" online. We didn't feel like we were part of a community. We met some great people, but we weren't experiencing that sense of belonging. Have you been there? It's hard.

We prayed for over a year for a community where we could share life with other believers. We visited some good churches and met some great people, but it never felt like "home."

One day we got invited over to someone's home with a group of people who wanted to start a new church in the area. I was elated. *Could this be our community? Was this our long-awaited answer to our many prayers?* I had such high expectations. My husband was out of town, so I ended up going by myself that night. I walked in the door and was greeted with friendly smiles and introductions, but it stopped there. The rest of the night I felt like I was in the middle of the room and no one even saw me. I was invisible. People talked right past me to others on the opposite side of the room. They laughed about inside jokes. I asked questions of others to try and get to know them. I truly wanted to know them. No one asked me a question. No one wanted to hear my story. I couldn't get out of there fast enough and cried all the way home. I wasn't seen, heard, or known and that felt awful. I was deflated. Hopes were dashed. Discouragement set in.

That night took me back to a season in my life when we had four little kids under the age of six. I felt lonely. I was pouring so much out and not getting much poured into me. I had good friends and wonderful neighbors who loved me but no one seemed to lean in during that season and ask how I was *really* doing.

Both circumstances made me ever more passionate to really see people—to care about what they care about. To hear their stories and ask deeper questions. To know them—the good, the messy, and the hard. When that happens there is connection. And deep down, that's what we all long for. These circumstances caused me to pray a heartfelt prayer:

Here I am, Lord. I'm available if You want to use me to make a difference in people's lives. Help me to see people and care about them. Help me to slow down enough to hear what they are really saying and what they really struggle with. Help me to know people and to help them know You. Help me to authentically connect with people so that they are drawn to You. Use mentoring as a way for people to be seen, heard, and known.

This book is an answer to that prayer.

The beautiful community we now have in Colorado is an answer to that prayer.

The ministry of MORE Mentoring that God has asked me to lead is an answer to that prayer.

All in His perfect timing.

MORE Mentoring

On an ordinary day in February 2014, I received an extraordinary call. I was sitting on my couch on a typical Saturday morning, spending time with Jesus just like I do on most mornings. I had nothing on my agenda. I was simply enjoying Him by praying, worshiping, dreaming, conversing, abiding, and dwelling. All of a sudden His presence became very real. You can't fully understand the manifest presence of God until you experience it. That day I experienced it!

It truly was as if Jesus showed up, sat next to me, and engaged in conversation with me. I pulled out my journal as He began speaking—not audibly—but very clearly into every fiber of my being. He was calling me to start a ministry called *MORE*. It was to be all about mentoring relationships, focused on prayer, so that people could come to know God as their Greatest Mentor.

My Bible was open to Ephesians 3 and 4, and verses 19-21 in chapter 3 jumped right out of the pages and straight into my heart: *And to know this love that suprasses knowledge that you may be filled to the measure of all the fullness of God. Now to Him who is able to do immeasurably more than all we could ask or imagine, according to his power that is at work within us, to him be glory in the church and in Christ Jesus through all generations, for ever and ever! Amen.*

This abundant life that Jesus came to give us is His greatest desire for us. It speaks of freedom, joy, and peace. His fullness is what we all desire but so few of us experience. It's His power at work in us that brings this about. Sometimes it's another person showing up, walking alongside us, and pointing us to Jesus that can give us a fuller understanding of what it looks like to live out the abundant life. That's why godly, prayerful mentors are so vital!

My heart was stirred. This calling on my life was confirmed on a couch yet the seed had been planted years earlier. Even the term "mentor" hadn't been used all that much until the last 10 years or so. I responded to the Lord by asking, "What does *MORE* stand for?"

Once again, I looked down at my Bible in chapter 4 of Ephesians. The words *one, unity, together,* and *fullness* flashed like neon lights. Jesus' desire is that we would be one like He and the Father and the Spirit are one. By coming together in mentoring relationships, we can experience oneness and fullness. The enemy hates unity and togetherness because it represents everything that God longs for us to experience . . . MORE of HIM.

This is what MORE stands for:

M - Mentoring (a form of discipleship focused on relationships)

O - One-to-one (care about the one; unity and coming together are of utmost importance)

R - Relating authentically (real and honest relationships are key)

E - Encouragement and prayer (these go hand in hand, with prayer as the very foundation)

In taking a step of faith to start the MORE Mentoring ministry, I started a prayer team. That was the best decision I could have ever made. We started out with 70 of my close friends and family members, then quickly grew to over 200. Today, we are seeing answers to prayers that were prayed all those years ago. I'm so grateful that when God calls, and we respond with, "Yes, Lord, here I am. I'm willing. Use me," He does.

That February day was like no other. I unexpectedly received a call from the Lord. For Moses it was a burning bush; for me it was a couch. I have experienced the "immeasurably more" ever since! What fun it has been to see the Lord bring others alongside me in this journey. We will never be the same.[1]

To be seen, heard, and known we need to come, be, and move.

The simplicity of mentoring can be narrowed down to these three words: Come. Be. Move. I've studied and prayed about these three words for a long time, and I believe they are foundational to our mentoring relationships. And so simple!

Come

Come with me. It's a personal invitation. It speaks of action, intentionality, and invitation. Come as you are. Come alongside. Come forward. Come available. Come teachable. Come together. Take a step toward another person.

---

1 *morementoring.org*

Be

Be who God made you to be. Share your story. Be OK with imperfection. Be filled to the measure of all the fullness of God. Let His power and influence overflow in and through your life.

Move

Move away from being stuck. Move out of the pit of despair, anxiety, and fear. Move forward. Move towards more of Jesus, more fullness of life, more freedom and joy. Move together. Move beyond what you could even imagine into the "immeasurably more."

PART 1

COME

CHAPTER 1

Come As You Are

My heart skipped a beat and my hands began to sweat as I read the letter I'd received in the mail. It was from a neighbor I had recently met.

She wrote, "Will you be my mentor?"

What in the world did she mean by that? What could I have to offer? Did she want me to teach her something? I'm not a teacher, and I certainly don't have counseling skills. What did she want from me?

I sank into a chair by the window, still holding the letter in my hands. I asked the Lord if this was something He wanted me to do. I quieted my heart to listen, and felt a God-confidence and courage sweep over me. Yes, I could do this *even though I have no idea what I'm doing.*

The next day, I called my neighbor Sarah to thank her for the letter and invite her over for coffee. While I waited for her, I pulled out a big pile of my favorite books and Bible studies. I arranged them on the coffee table, hoping something might interest her. When she arrived, we strolled past the books to the kitchen where I poured two cups of coffee. Then we carried our mugs to the sun porch and we sat down to chat—for an hour.

Sarah poured out her fears one after the other. She confessed her nervousness about her oldest child entering kindergarten and went on to ask how I'd handled sending my kids off to school for the first time. How did I get through the days with a houseful of small children? How did I find time for myself and for my husband, much less time for my relationship with Jesus? On and on the questions flowed.

I answered her questions as best I could by simply sharing my story. I then suggested we pray. As I prayed for Sarah, I could relate to her fears as a young mom. I've been there, and I know how hard it can be. I asked Jesus to meet her needs and give her His peace. As we prayed and surrendered Sarah's (and my) concerns to God, the pressure began to lift from my anxious heart. Peace filled me as Jesus showed me that I didn't need to take on her burdens or have the solutions for her. That's what *He* does!

Very quickly it became clear what my neighbor meant when she said she wanted a mentor. She was longing for someone to talk with who was just a little "further down the road"—in mothering, in marriage, in walking with Jesus. She could get all those how-to books and Bible studies in other places. What she needed was someone to love her, listen to her, encourage her, and pray with her.

That was the beginning of the most delightful journey of mentoring with Sarah. I still consider her one of my best friends to this day. During that season of mentoring, I listened and encouraged, sharing from my own journey. Together, we did a lot of praying. And we began to experience God's miraculous answers to our expectant, united prayers. Sarah grew in her confidence as a mother and in her faith. I grew in my confidence as a mentor through the assurance that Jesus provides the answers—and I don't have to.

> **"I grew in my confidence as a mentor through the assurance that Jesus provides the answers—and I don't have to."**

The realization hit me: this really is quite basic and yet so powerful! Mentoring doesn't need to be some big, scary deal. It's not that complicated. Effective mentoring can be as easy as talking and praying together. And the best part is: prayer-focused mentoring changes lives. Mine included.

When I received Sarah's letter, I had no idea what being a mentor looked like or what she expected of me. I didn't feel qualified to teach or advise, if that's what she was thinking. When I realized she simply wanted to spend time with me, to observe how I do life, and that Jesus would meet our needs through prayer, I was freed to be myself and let her come along with me. As I modeled what I'd already experienced—in mothering, in my personal spiritual life, my life in general—she watched and learned, not from any kind of expert, but from an ordinary woman who just happened to be a little bit ahead in her life's journey.

As Sarah and I moved forward together in our mentoring relationship, both of us benefitted. In the beginning, I lived my life as I normally did and invited Sarah to join me along the way. We'd meet occasionally, go for walks, and visit over coffee on my porch. Nothing required a lot of work or preparation for either one of us. Over time, Sarah learned from my example. And because I wanted to be a good mentor, I became even more diligent in my daily time with Jesus. As our friendship matured, our conversations and prayer times deepened. We both ended up growing.

Here's how Sarah describes our time together:

"I'd watch my neighbor Nancy take walks with her husband and interact with her kids. Her daughter became my children's first babysitter. As a young mom with small children, I was most struck by the fact that Nancy loved her four children so very much, but she did not *worry*. How did this loving mom have so much *peace*?

"I kept feeling a prompting from the Lord to ask Nancy to be my mentor. I had all my excuses why not to do this. I thought, *Nancy is so busy, she has four children of her own!* I also thought, *She is such a godly woman that she must be mentoring several other women right now.* I didn't want to bother her. But the prompting from the Lord did not cease, so I chose to obey.

"I wrote Nancy a letter, sharing with her all the fruit from the Lord I could see in her life and asked her if she would consider mentoring me. I felt nervous, like I was asking too much of her. (I've since joked with Nancy, 'I kind of felt the pressure like I was proposing to you!')

"I was so surprised and excited when Nancy answered with a 'Yes!' She said she was not mentoring anyone else right now, and I was thrilled I obeyed the Lord.

"Nancy was so loving, encouraging, and the best listener. I felt like I could share intimate things because I trusted her and was not judged by her. She always pointed me to God's Word. I never left my time with her without praying together.

"Nancy truly taught me how to pray. And that is what changes everything! She would pray so beautifully, specifically, and expectantly, and then be so patient while encouraging me to pray. I learned about the power of praying in agreement together.

"I loved getting to know Nancy more as she would also share with me how I could pray for her. We would pray each week specifically over our marriages, our children, and many other details and decisions of our lives. There is nothing more bonding than to pray and rejoice together when God so faithfully answers.

"Because Nancy took that one-on-one intentional time with me, I now feel comfortable to pray with others. She taught me the best thing to do is have a prayer partner and to pray with other women. I think of Nancy each Monday morning as women gather in my home and I lead a prayer group. I can do this because Nancy taught me how and nurtured my faith and confidence.

"I am now better equipped to say yes to ministries God is calling me to. I serve as a leader in another Christian ministry and am now moving into a prayer coordinator role in women's ministry at my church. And even more importantly, Nancy taught me how to be a praying wife and a praying mom. My family, too, is impacted in this life and into eternity!

> *We all have something to offer in every season of our lives.*

"Because I obeyed God's prompting and Nancy was willing to be my mentor, I am forever changed and forever grateful."

We all have something to offer in every season of our lives. Do you believe that? I sure do! You don't need to be any kind of great leader or be in the senior citizen season of life to make a great mentor. You don't need to have your life all figured out before you can step into somebody else's life and invest in her and share what you are learning. Come as you are. You can be yourself and trust Jesus to work through you.

Our relational God speaks it to us throughout the Bible many times and in creative ways.

Your God will come . . . He will come to save you (Isaiah 35:4b).

Come near me and listen . . . (Isaiah 48:16a).

Come to me, all who are weary and burdened, and I will give you rest (Matthew 11:28).

God longs to come to us in His fullness, strength, and power. And He longs for us to come to Him, to give Him our surrendered life and to receive His rest, His freedom, His joy, and His peace.

He also calls us to come together. He didn't create us to live isolated lives.

Let them all come together and take their stand . . . (Isaiah 44:11b).

And one standing alone can be attacked and defeated, but two can stand back-to-back and conquer . . . (Ecclesiastes 4:12a, TLB).

I especially love the word "come" as it relates to mentoring. Both mentee and mentor take a step towards each other—come forward, come available, come teachable. And we invite God to come with us. As we take the intentional steps to come together, with a sincere desire to grow closer to God, He will do beautiful things in our lives.

> *"As we take the intentional steps to come together, with a sincere desire to grow closer to God, He will do beautiful things in our lives."*

The simple words "come with me" might mean going out to lunch together, or inviting someone into your home for a visit, or just having a conversation on the phone. "Come with me" says "I want to get to know you. Let's start there."

Just come.

CHAPTER 2

Come Alongside

There's a story in the Bible that has gripped my heart in recent years. It's a mirror of sorts, revealing the heart of Jesus for mentors today.

In Matthew 9, we read about Jesus traveling through towns and villages, teaching in the synagogues and proclaiming the good news of the Kingdom. In His compassion He heals their diseases and sicknesses. He can see how harassed and helpless the people are, and that they need help. And here's the kicker: Jesus tells His disciples to ask God—"the Lord of the harvest"— to send out more workers. In other words, there weren't enough hands to tend to all the people who needed Jesus and His help.

When it comes to mentoring, this same scenario seems to be playing out today, both in our communities and in many of our churches. Many people, often young women, long for mentors who cannot be found. I hear from potential mentees all the time, "Where can I find a mentor?" Some of these young women are going through difficult times and they crave the nurturing of a more mature woman. Some are beginning new seasons of life and yearn for a mentor to come alongside them as they face the unknown. Others are already thriving spiritually, full of life and enthusiasm, with a genuine desire to learn from a mentor who is a little more spiritually established. These potential mentees aren't looking for a *perfect* mentor; they are just looking for a *present* one.

> *These potential mentees aren't looking for a perfect mentor; they are just looking for a present one.*

When MORE Mentoring began, we consistently heard from women *looking for* mentors, and not as many women *stepping up to be* a mentor. I wonder if this imbalance is because so many potential mentors don't realize how much they have to offer, or don't know how to be a mentor or what it all involves. Perhaps we've created a mentoring monster in our minds, apprehensive of the potential pitfalls we might encounter if we agree to become a mentor (more on this in Chapter 4). Regardless of the reason for a shortage of mentors, Jesus' words are clear: "The harvest is plentiful. Where are the workers?"

This Scripture isn't intended to heap guilt on us. That only happens when we put the focus in the wrong place—when we put pressure on ourselves instead of trying to grasp the situation from Jesus' perspective. We feel shame when we look at how much work there is to do and at our hesitancy—or full-blown unwillingness—to step up. But when we look at the harvest through Jesus' compassionate eyes, we see people who are harassed and helpless. When we look around and take notice, we see exhausted young moms, college students clinging to their faith, weary wives who need a word of encouragement. We see lonely widows, stressed-out professionals, single women eager to find the love of their lives or at the very least move on with their lives.

"To be a mentor, all you need is the willingness to be what I like to call a come-alongsider."

Imagine simply coming alongside one of these women, to help her reach Jesus, to encourage her to stay close to Him. We can all do that! And thankfully, more and more women are rising to the mentoring challenge every day. A mentoring movement is emerging.

To be a mentor, all you need is the willingness to be what I like to call a *come-alongsider*.

When I was a senior in high school, the mother of one of my best friends passed away. I sat with my friend Lisa and cried with her. I had no experience in coming alongside someone in the depths of their grief. I didn't have answers. I had no idea what I should say or not say, so most of the time I just listened and let her process.

All those years ago, the term "mentor" wasn't common, but Lisa now calls me her mentor. Here's how she describes that season:

"Before I even lost my mom, God knew what I would need. One of those needs was a true and faithful friend to walk beside

"SOMETIMES, BEING A MENTOR IS ABOUT YOUR AGE, YOUR EXPERIENCES, OR YOUR KNOWLEDGE.

BUT MORE OFTEN THAN NOT IT'S ABOUT CARING AND SHOWING UP."

me, to listen but not necessarily fix things (obviously losing my mom could not be fixed). What Nancy offered to me was a safe place to just be . . . be sad, be confused, and sometimes just be goofy. Being present and being real was her greatest gift. I knew nothing about being a Christian, but I watched how Nancy lived out her faith. Looking back all these years later, I can see this was when the foundation of my faith was laid."

As a teenager, I didn't have a clue what I was doing. I was just a come-alongsider for a friend in her season of need. I can't take any credit for what God did in my friend's life. He worked through me, as unprepared as I was. That was a growing time for both Lisa and me.

Sometimes, being a mentor is about your age, your experiences, or your knowledge. But more often than not it's about caring and showing up. Mentors can often feel like we don't have the right answers and won't know what to say, but if we look at mentoring as being someone who merely comes alongside another, it doesn't seem so daunting. We point our mentees to Jesus through prayer and remind them of who He is. It's as simple as that.

Mentoring begins with a simple invitation to come, like we talked about in Chapter 1. My neighbor reached out to me, asking me to be her mentor. But I have to ask myself: What if I had noticed her first? Did I see how she wrestled groceries to her door, toddlers in tow? Did I notice how tired and worried she looked when we ran into each other on the sidewalk? I think that's part of what Jesus was trying to tell His disciples when He said, "Look at the harvest!" Look around us. Who can benefit from our presence, from our commitment to come alongside for a season?

Once we identify a potential mentee, the invitation to come alongside her can start with a casual invitation for coffee or a quick visit to deliver her a taste of that new recipe we've been wanting to try. Women love it when we reach out. We begin the conversation and see where God takes it from there. Perhaps a mentoring relationship will happen immediately, or it may take a while, or it may not happen at all. We don't need to force anything. All we need to do is open the door to a relationship.

> *We all need people to walk beside—to encourage and pour into each other.*

God loves when His people come together. Relationship is part of His very nature. The Trinity is our perfect example—God the Father, God the Son, God the Spirit—three and yet one, in perfect unity. In His image, we were created for relationship, for togetherness, for oneness.

The older we get, the more we realize that in every season of life we need horizontal relationships with others alongside our vertical relationship with Christ. We all need people to walk beside—to encourage and pour into each other. Yes, we know that God is enough in our lives, and that if we had no one else but Him, He would be enough. But in His beautiful plan, He designed for us to be in relationship with others.

It should be no surprise then that Satan tries to keep us isolated, alone, and disconnected. God warned us about this all the way back in the garden of Eden when He said, "It is not good for man to be alone" (Genesis 2:18). Living solo is not His best for us. That doesn't mean He guarantees a spouse for every human or that singleness isn't His plan. It *does* mean He knows we each require the lifegiving components of community and the companionship of coming alongside others. That's His plan.

God is all about togetherness, including His promise to always be with us. Multiple times throughout the Bible, God speaks the words "I will be with you" to fearful, anxious, overwhelmed, and discouraged people. His name Emmanuel translates to "God With Us." Jesus came to this earth to be with us, and after He ascended to heaven, He promised He would still be with us in the form of the Holy Spirit.

Following His example, here's my question for us today: What if we, as God's people, who have the Holy Spirit within us, start being more intentional about saying to anxious mentees, "I will be with you"? What could happen when we make ourselves available, and instead of doing a lot of talking, we listen and pray, asking the Holy Spirit to intervene? How about just drawing close, willing and present, in the midst of their rough seasons as well as in their ordinary times of everyday life? What if we noticed people and cared enough to say, "I want to come alongside you"?

This is what so much of what mentoring is all about. It's a "with you movement," and it starts with one person caring about another one. Voicing the very important words, "I will be with you," and then coming alongside another person will change lives.

CHAPTER 3

Real Needs

Linda saw a lot of real needs around her as she served at her church and decided it was time to take action.

"When I began serving at Berean Baptist Church as their Women's Ministry Leader there was no mentoring ministry. We were a large, growing church with many opportunities for women to connect in Bible Studies, small groups, and serving ministries, but we had no opportunities for them to connect one to one. As I met and talked with many women, the same need kept surfacing—the need for one-to-one genuine relationships.

"In a world where lives are directed and displayed on social media, women have hundreds, even thousands, of Facebook, Instagram, and other multi-media connections. But they have no one with whom they can have a genuine, authentic relationship.

It became very clear that we are living in a culture afflicted by relational poverty. As women shared their lives I found they were lonely, isolated, anxious, feeling invisible, fearful, depressed, and disconnected.

> **It became very clear that we are living in a culture afflicted by relational poverty.**

"They desired someone to journey with them below the surface of their exterior façade. Someone to care for, to love them where they were at, someone to walk through their unique season of life. Someone who has perhaps walked the same journey a season before . . . and come out on the other side . . . strong.

"I began praying and asking God to connect me with women who had a heart for mentoring as I did. He brought six women to be on the Leadership Team. We met monthly and began our search for a mentoring ministry that would meet the needs of the women we serve and be a good fit for the biblically centered, prayer-focused, multi-generational culture at Berean.

"In God's faithfulness and perfect timing, He answered our prayers and delivered MORE Mentoring ministry into our hands. MORE met every need and more (no pun intended) of what we were looking for. This all happened in January 2020, and then COVID hit. In the weeks that followed, the church was closed and we were confined to our homes. Our team began to meet weekly online as we heard feedback from desperate women. Their (literal) cries for help and their need for another woman to walk through that challenging, isolating time…moved us to get the ministry up and running (via Zoom) by June 1. God led us through every step of the process, parting the seas of COVID constraints!

"Each mentoring relationship looks as unique as the women God pairs with each other. We've had women of all ages placed together, we have grandmothers mentoring their granddaughters, older women mentoring younger, younger women who have journeyed with the Lord longer paired with an older woman desiring to know more. Some mentors are mentoring family members, extended family members, neighbors, co-workers, women mentoring remotely online with a friend in another state. Women are mentoring in their homes, coffee shops, and parks—the opportunities for relationship are endless.

"Most importantly . . . God is being glorified through it all . . . as one woman walks alongside another with Jesus in the middle . . . as each woman grows deeper in her love for the Lord and relationship with each other. It's beautiful to witness . . . it's true fellowship, discipleship, prayer, and worship to our Lord."

When it comes right down to it, the real need for each one of us is relationship. Most people who long for a mentor these days are feeling alone and disconnected. Many feel anxious and overwhelmed, unsure of what lies ahead and how to navigate it.

Ironically, the Internet and online platforms connect our global society unlike anything we've ever experienced in the history of the world. So why do so many people still feel disconnected? Why are we so lonely and uncertain about our place in the world?

Because social media isn't real life.

Our needs for authentic connection can't possibly be fulfilled through funny memes on Facebook or flattering pictures on Instagram. I'm amazed at how many times I've seen people post multiple pictures on social media that made all seem well, until I actually talked with them and learned they were in the middle of something really hard. The online pictures didn't line up with reality.

> *Social media can give us a false sense of connection.*

Social media can give us a false sense of connection. People can read what we have to say or listen to our opinions on a current debate, but they can't really know our heart behind those words. Video calls connect us admittedly better than faceless phone calls of the past, but even those calls can't satisfy the longing for a good, old-fashioned hug.

In addition, news broadcasts tend to highlight stories that breed fear, uncertainty, and discouragement. The onslaught of constant online information (or rumors) can overwhelm even the strongest person. No, for sure, social media isn't real life.

Real life is boots on the ground, hands on—you and me together in the face of it all.

At the time of this writing, people have never been more isolated, lonely, disconnected, anxious, depressed, and fearful. Mental health issues are becoming a pandemic of their own. We are hearing of suicides, violence, and division being at an all-time high. Outward violence stems from inner loneliness and disconnection. It's a way of being noticed, a crying out for connection.

Real life. Real needs.

We've got to break this cycle of relational disconnection.

In real life, we *all* have real needs. Some are very basic: a need to be loved; a need to be valued or accepted. As human beings we all need real community, real relationships, and real conversation. None of us is exempt—not even the most devoted introvert, truth be told. Like it or not, God created us with the need for one another.

As recent as the 1990s, much of our connection as Christians happened within our churches. We attended Sunday school, Sunday evening and mid-week services, and gathered for ice cream or pizza afterwards. We picnicked and fellowshipped and hosted seasonal gatherings, purely for the purpose of spending time together. To be fair, many churches still do these sorts of activities and are committed to fostering close relationships. But the harsh reality is that attendees, notably our young people, are leaving the church in droves. The statistics are shocking.[2] Could part of this exodus be happening because we're losing the feeling of belonging as an integral part to a vibrant, interactive church community? I understand there are many, many reasons for this downward spiral within the church, but I can't help but wonder how much can be attributed to the lack of genuine relationship.

> **"As human beings we all need real community, real relationships, and real conversation."**

---

2   *https://www.barna.com/research/resilient-disciples/*

Mentoring is an answer. It's a solution for these great needs. We engage others in a sincere conversation, asking questions and paying attention to the answers. We ask them to share their story. Power is released when we say to another individual, with genuine interest, "I want to hear your story." As mentors, we open the door to communication and, with hope, to a relationship that can advance to connect at the heart level.

That's why mentoring is so needed in our world today. Mentoring moves us from being detached and disconnected to being together. And there is great power in this type of connection. It cultivates unity and strength, meeting some of our innermost needs—especially when we are talking about Jesus-centered, Scripture-based, prayer-focused mentoring that results in life-changing moments.

My heart goes out to ministry leaders and church leaders today who shepherd a large group of needy people. The weight can feel so great! How do we carry so many burdens? We don't have to do it alone. We find others who are mentors in our local churches and ministries to help share those burdens. They are the people who lean into the hard stuff, who aren't afraid to step in and be available.

To experience this type of mentoring, we need to learn a little more so we can truly see, hear, and know the mentees who desperately need and long for a mentor.

"MENTORING MOVES US FROM BEING DETACHED AND DISCONNECTED TO BEING TOGETHER."

Let's take a closer look at Gen Z for a moment, the generation born between 1997 and 2012. I've heard them referred to as the lost generation. The majority are unchurched and don't read the Bible. Yet, an article from the Christian Post states: "Though the majority of Gen Z is not engaged in scriptural study and in a distrustful relationship with the religious institutions, they are eager for trusted adults, including religious leaders, to invest in their lives."[3]

They may not even know it, but deep down, I believe they want to know God and be in relationship with Him. They're looking for someone to show them how to know Jesus, how to pray effectively, better understand the Bible, become more Christ-like. These young people ache to discover their life's purpose, to have assurance their life can make—is making—a difference. They don't want to waste their days, but long to be about something bigger than themselves. Against popular opinion, this younger generation really does want to have an impact on other people's lives. Mostly, they want to be needed and pursued, to gain confidence and boldness. Don't we all have a need for that?

The article goes on to explain the dynamics of a study that collected data from more than 10,000 surveys and 150 interviews with kids from Gen Z. The study found, "Today's young people are also the 'loneliest of any generation.'"[4]

---

3   *https://www.christianpost.com/news/gen-z-craves-spiritual-mentoring-new-study-finds*

4   *https://www.christianpost.com/news/gen-z-craves-spiritual-mentoring-new-study-finds*

What I found particularly fascinating is how many young people agreed with the statement, "I am more likely to listen to adults in my life if I know that they care about me." Younger generations desperately need and desire mentors who will walk with them and encourage them. They need people who will speak the truth in love, but even more than that, they need someone who cares.

Can you imagine what might happen if more of us nurtured these young mentoring relationships? It is staggering to think of the impact we could have on the next generation. But the younger generation isn't the only one with needs for authentic connection. I think we can safely say that every generation around the world has its own set of needs that could be met if only someone made himself or herself available.

Most of us are familiar with how God called Abraham, Moses, and Samuel. You can read their stories in Genesis 22:11, Exodus 3:4, and 1 Samuel 3:10.

What's so interesting to me is that God called their names twice *and* used exclamation points. It was like God was saying, "Make sure you don't miss this. Pay attention. I'm speaking to YOU!"

In all three situations, those being called responded, "Here I am." The words "here I am" speak of availability and surrender. Going all in. Setting all else down. Wholeheartedly following God's call.

When I think of people today who are the "here I am" kind of people, I immediately think of first responders—those who are willing to give up their lives on behalf of another life. They are not afraid to run towards someone who needs their help, rather than run the other direction.

I see mentors as the spiritual first responders of our day. When crisis hits, when a person cries for help, when a member of a younger generation reaches out for guidance, mentors step forward with courage, boldness, and a "here I am" attitude. Mentors see the needs of others and are willing to set aside their own desires to step in. Mentors are the heroes, the champions who are making a difference.

I have a champion like this in my own life, and I'm so grateful she answered with a "here I am" attitude. My mentor is Fern Nichols, Founder of Moms In Prayer International, (formerly Moms In Touch).[5] I had been quite involved in the ministry of Moms In Prayer and was privileged to be around Fern up close, as well as watch her speak on stage. I heard her talk about her relationship with God and watched her model what it looks like to live a joyful, peaceful, abundant life. She is the most gracious, encouraging, godly person I know. Fern Nichols is well known around the world, and I was convinced this well-respected woman would have no time for me.

> *I see mentors as the spiritual first responders of our day.*

The first time I reached out to her to ask her to be my mentor, she didn't answer the phone and I didn't leave a message. I chickened out and waited *six whole years* to make that phone call again. This time she answered, and she so graciously agreed to mentor me.

---

5   *momsinprayer.org*

Since we live in different states, we connect via a monthly phone call. We have deep conversations, ask each other questions, and we always pray together. I leave those phone calls feeling loved and connected, and more in love with Jesus because Fern is so in love with Jesus. Her fullness overflows to me and as a result, I'm a changed person. Now that's "mentoring made real" in action.

So what can we, as the body of Christ, do to address the real needs of those around us? We can come together. With a united purpose we can reach out and connect with an unlimited number of other people with real needs, just like us.

Genuine Concerns

One cool summer morning, my friend and I sat around my kitchen table drinking hot tea and sharing stories. Like me, she is also the mom of young adult kids, so we have much in common. As the conversation shifted to mentoring, she voiced some of her concerns. Real concerns. I've heard them before.

"I don't know, Nancy," my friend confessed. "To be honest, I am enjoying my free time right now. Please don't judge me, but I don't really want to be a mentor."

She continued with a teasing smile. "I mean, what if my mentee sucks the life out of me? You know? That could happen. Plus, after a lifetime of raising kids it's kind of nice being self-absorbed." At that she giggled, and I did too. I know my friend well enough to know she's not a selfish person. She has a heart full of compassion.

Then her mood shifted. She became almost somber. "Seriously, I devoted so much of my life to parenting, and quite frankly, things didn't end up the way I'd hoped they would. I don't really think I'm qualified to mentor anyone. I tried so hard to train my kids to follow Jesus. If their faith hasn't remained strong, how can I hope to do better with other young people? I feel like such a failure and so unworthy."

The hurt in my friend's eyes tugged at my heart. So many moms I know are experiencing this same heartache as they watch their young adult children turn away from the values of their upbringing.

"What if I say or do the wrong things?" my friend asked me. "Or what if a mentee has expectations of me that I can't deliver, and she ends up rejecting the truth? I feel bad, but I'm not going to lie—I'm afraid I can't do it."

As my friend spilled her sincere concerns, I could see how the enemy was burdening her with heaviness that wasn't hers to carry. I know she has been a good mother, and still is. She is far from a failure, but past wounds have left scars of inadequacy. I think many of us can say this is true of our lives as well. How many of us suffer from insecurity and fear because of past experiences? I know I sure have.

I remember the feelings of shortcoming that swept over me when I received that note in the mail from my neighbor. How could I be her mentor? I didn't know enough. My life was messy. I had issues. If she really knew me deep down, would she still want me as her mentor? Insecurity reared its ugly head for me, too. My friend isn't alone.

I applauded my friend's courage for being so honest with me, assuring her I hold no judgment and that, in fact, I get it. She assured me she would take her feelings of unworthiness to God and maybe, "just maybe," she said, "take the risk of mentoring."

The real concern of not feeling worthy threatens many qualified women when they consider becoming mentors. Often the word "mentor" can be intimidating; the expectations seem way beyond who we think we are or what we can offer.

I've heard so many times, "I can't do it."

To which I reply, "Yes you can and here's why!"

Let's look at Moses's life for a moment. He was a great leader and yet stayed so humble. He had an

> *The real concern of not feeling worthy threatens many qualified women when they consider becoming mentors.*

amazing, close relationship with God. They talked face to face. A whole nation followed Moses as he followed God. He was a mentor to many. No pressure there!

When God called Moses to lead the Israelites out of Egypt into the Promised Land,[6] Moses felt:

Insecure

Moses's struggle: Who am I?

God's response: I will be with you.

---

6 See Exodus 3:11–4:15.

Intimidated

> Moses's struggle: What if they don't believe me or listen to me?

> God's response: What is that in your hand? I've equipped you and provided for your needs.

Inadequate

> Moses's struggle: I have never been eloquent. I am slow of speech and tongue.

> God's response: I will help you speak and will teach you what to say.

Insignificant

> Moses's struggle: Pardon Your servant, Lord; please send someone else.

> God's response: I will send Aaron with you. I will help both of you speak and will teach you what to do.

Notice that Moses's concerns focused on himself and not on God. We tend to do the same, don't we? "I can't. I'm not able. I'm not good enough." We place ourselves in our own way—our own worst enemy, so to speak. We forget that "I AM WHO I AM" is with us. We need to replace "Who am I" with "I AM WHO."

Let's take a moment to expose what else holds us back—the obstacles that cause us to resist mentoring. To make you feel better, I want to assure you that most mentors have to work through some of these concerns at one point or another. So, yep, you're not alone either.

Fear

Over the years many of the mentors I've worked with admit that, before they started mentoring, they felt the fear of being unqualified, inadequate, insufficient, not equipped, or intimidated. Sound familiar? Just like Moses and my honest friend, many of us have these concerns when we face a new responsibility, especially when there are unknowns involved. I've had to remind myself more than once when I'm being stretched and put in a position of being uncomfortable and of not knowing what the outcome will be, "Do it scared. Do it anyway. See what God can do." On the other side of that wall of fear is our influence. Keep speaking God's truth and let God deal with it. Some mentees will listen, and some won't, but their response is not our responsibility. We do the pouring. God does the work.

What Ifs

What if my mentor and I don't click? What if she clings to me? What if nothing happens and the relationship turns into a dud? What if I make mistakes? Just like no parent is free from mistakes, we as mentors will make mistakes as well. We can count on it. That's when we rely on Jesus being the Gap-Filler. When we are weak, He is strong. When we don't know what to say, we listen to the Holy Spirit and ask Him to show us what to say. We do our best, and trust Jesus to fill in the gaps.

The "what ifs" are endless if we allow ourselves to get sucked down that path. Dare to turn the "what ifs" around. Instead of dwelling on the negative "what ifs," consider the positive outcomes. What if your mentoring relationship blossoms and a woman's life is changed forever? What if a desperate person's life becomes full of Jesus? What if a life is saved? Think of the possibilities!

Expectations

To address my friend's specific concern, for her and anyone else with her same pain, I want to point out that mentoring is not the same as parenting. Mentors agree to invest into the life of another person who wants their input, who is seeking their influence. As mentors, we don't discipline or counsel; we come alongside and we pray. Unlike parent and child, mentoring relationships do not last forever; they are designed for a season.

One of the main questions I get asked regarding expectations is, "How long do I need to mentor someone? Is this a long-term thing?" I like to put potential mentors at ease by assuring them that mentoring relationships can end in a timely fashion, and they can end well.

One way to set up proper expectations in the beginning is to agree to go through one mentoring guide together. That opens the door to end the mentoring relationship and provides the opportunity to move on to another mentee. Listen to the Spirit and follow His guidance. You may stick it out a whole lot longer with your mentee if you believe God is calling you to follow His lead. Typically, in a church mentoring ministry we encourage mentors and mentees to meet every other week and to have check-ins every six months or so to see if they should continue on. After three years, the mentor should encourage the mentee to become a mentor. That's a good goal to have.

Organic vs. Structured Mentoring

Some people assume structured mentoring is too forced and that mentoring relationships that happen naturally, or organically, are better. The more I've talked with church leaders, the more I've heard that roughly 10% of their people are stepping into organic mentoring relationships. They don't need help. They are pursuing each other on their own and needs are being met. That leaves 90% who desire a mentoring relationship, but who need a little help getting started or equipped with some good tools to make mentoring become more natural.

> *"I applaud those of you who are out there living out a mentoring lifestyle and doing it really well."*

I applaud those of you who are out there living out a mentoring lifestyle and doing it really well. I'm your #1 cheerleader. We need more of you!

For those in the 90% range, we at MORE Mentoring are here to help you, encourage you, support you. We have written mentoring guides[7] to equip you on this mentoring journey. We want to pour into you so you can pour into others. As our team comes alongside the local church, we help provide them with some preliminary structure that leads to a lot of freedom. Structured mentoring is the starting place that grows into organic mentoring—from a ministry to a movement.

God is here to help us overcome our obstacles just as He was with Moses. God says: I will be with you. I've equipped you and

7   morementoring.org/resources

provided for your needs. I will help you speak and will teach you what to say and what to do.

May we get past our real concerns, past ourselves, and turn to the great I AM who is more than enough in us.

CHAPTER 4

Real Purpose

One fateful mid-morning, Angelica's beloved big brother was killed in a single-engine plane crash. At the age of 30, he entered his heavenly home, leaving behind his wife and four little children, one not yet born. He also left his little sister behind in indescribable grief.

One week later, Angelica's older friend Sheila lost her son Zachary to cancer. He was 33 years old and had suffered intensely at the ravages of cancer. Watching him suffer and then the final goodbye shattered Sheila's heart and mind.

Sheila and Angelica shared a heartache. Both their worlds had been turned upside down.

The two friends—of two different generations—cried together, shared painful days and crushing agony, and shared how God showed up in little and big ways. Then they cried again at how good God is and that He is trustworthy and true and faithful. It is an honor to walk with someone in her anguish and be invited into her real life—into the places of heartbreak and misery. It's not pretty or easy or put together, but it's precious.

This is not the story Sheila or Angelica would have written for their lives, for sure. The journey was hard and still is hard, yet Sheila shares the experience of God walking beside her.

"It's not like I thought it would be. Not full of miracles of healing or happiness and comfort to my heart. Instead, it was the constant presence of Him catching my tears and singing songs of tender love over me. It felt like I was alone during that time, except for God. And every time a person stepped into my path to carry the load, it was like God placed him or her there. Sharing this time with Angelica was such an example of receiving God's comfort through others."

Shortly after Zach's homegoing, Sheila felt most comfortable around "the broken people," as she calls them. And she discovered they were everywhere.

"I hadn't seen them before my loss with as much compassion as I do now. We don't always have the endurance for other people's battles with sorrow or the understanding of the lifelong hole in your heart that causes you to limp. In the past, I would try to fix them or help them instead of loving them and listening. Touching lives with those who are suffering reminds me that all the things in this world, not just my world, are broken. It continually lifts my eyes to the One who makes all things new. He redeems. He restores."

"THERE IS A PURPOSE IN OUR PAIN THAT FOLDS INTO THE

GREATER

PURPOSE"

FOR OUR LIVES.

Both Sheila and Angelica have experienced the purpose that comes with extreme grief and pain. Sheila is still drawn to the hurting and the messy, and she mentors others because she knows what it's like. In truth, we all desperately need God's touch on our lives, whether that comes through trauma and suffering or through some other means. Nothing is wasted in God's divine wisdom. There is a purpose in our pain that folds into the greater purpose for our lives.

Did you know we all have a purpose for our lives? The general calling for every one of us as believers in Christ is found in Matthew 28:19. These were some of Jesus' very last words before He left this earth: "Therefore go and make disciples of all nations." In His infinite wisdom, He calls us all. I'm so glad He didn't tell us exactly how to do it. It's also a good thing He doesn't restrict His command to those who have no personal problems, or none of us would qualify.

And let me add, He also doesn't say to do this only while we're young, or for just those limited few energetic years during the prime of our lives. Our purpose doesn't expire. I've heard from women who are empty nesters or retired, and who now believe their lives no longer have a significant purpose. The contrary is true. You do indeed have a purpose and others need you!

"You do indeed have a purpose and others need you!"

Those of us who are older, who have walked with Jesus for years, have experienced more life and gleaned more wisdom than our younger counterparts. Each of us has something to offer to a following generation that is eager to learn. You may think your role is very small, but I want you to know, it is so vital and can make a great difference in someone's life, especially for a younger woman who desperately wants to learn from you.

Generational Differences

Sometimes when we discuss generational differences, it can feel like we are putting people in a box or putting a label on them. Bear with me. I think it's an important discussion to have so we can gain a healthy perspective of those who live in different generations. To help us understand each other better, let's break down some of the more noticeable differences between our generations.

We could talk in depth about all the different generations and what makes them unique, but to keep this simple let's call these two generations a Mentee and a Mentor.

Typically, a mentee is in her 20s, 30s, or 40s. Now, to be sure, a mentee can be any age. We've seen 60-year-old mentees as well as budding 20-something mentors, but right now we're describing the most common profile of a mentee.

Here are the typical characteristics of today's 20-, 30-, or 40-year-old mentee: She is relational. Connection is very important. Community is important. Loneliness is real. She just wants a relationship. She wants to connect heart-to-heart. That is super important to her. I love that about those mentees!

Mentees are also plagued by stress in today's world. They're seeking a warm, caring environment. They're in the middle of making important life decisions. They're often very anxious or fearful about what's ahead. The younger generation wants truth, and they will keep searching until they find it rather than naively accepting what they've been told.

A mentee also desires to process hurts or frustrations with others. She is an open book. She is often willing to pour it all out and verbally process inside information with a mentor. She will be open about her issues. She doesn't hold those back. That's a great quality in mentees.

> **The younger generation wants truth, and they will keep searching until they find it rather than naively accepting what they've been told.**

Now let's look at what a mentor typically looks like. A mentor is in her 50s, 60s, or older. As of the writing of this book, most mentors matured during the "pre-digital age." I laughed when I first heard that term because it sounds like a pre-dinosaur age. (Don't take that personally, mentors. I'm right there with you.) So much of the current digital age is about technology. The younger generation carries their phones in their hip pocket and they use them to manage their lives. Typically, as mentors, we're not as likely to manage our lives digitally, but we're learning. We still like paper calendars (at least one tucked in somewhere, if only for old times' sake) and have been known to write checks instead of paying electronically.

We're maybe not on social media like our mentees are. We prefer to meet in person, face-to-face, and that's OK—good, in fact. Most mentors grew up in a culture that kept things private. There was no Facebook to share our lives so publicly, and besides, it was no one else's business. Consequently, mentors might be more reserved and less apt to share deeply and openly.

The generational difference is so interesting as I look at my own life. I was born in January 1965, so as of 2022, I am right smack dab in the middle. Mentees, I get you. Mentors, I get you. I have one foot in both worlds.

I understand technology, but I also value meeting in person. I have online connections as well as friends I look forward to connecting with at the local coffee shop. There are some parts of my life I'm eager to post online, and other intimacies I'll keep to myself.

As I consider both generations, I call on those of us who are in the mentoring generation to embrace our younger counterparts. Let's be eager to embrace the following generations, one person at a time, to understand how she's feeling and where she's coming from. Having that understanding will be a tremendous help to us as mentors. As we gain a more accurate perspective of the younger generation, it can help us in other areas of our lives.

> *"Let's be eager to embrace the following generations, one person at a time, to understand how she's feeling and where she's coming from."*

As I've come alongside churches and mentors, I hear from many women who don't see themselves as mentors. And I think it's even more true for men. So many men in my life think this way, even though they would make awesome mentors, in my opinion. Sometimes we all need a little reminding of this high calling on our lives.

For those of you dear readers who don't feel needed, be assured there is some other person who needs your hard-fought wisdom, who will treasure your time and your prayers.

To our mentors who are further down the road than us—we celebrate you! You have a purpose that is worth more than gold.

When Jesus tells us to "make disciples," He doesn't give step-by-step instructions or one specific way to go about it. If we consider the fact that a disciple is a learner, then a mentee is a disciple. I believe with all my heart the most effective form of discipleship is one-on-one, or life-on-life. Mentorship is a form of discipleship. One church goes so far as to describe mentorship as "1:1 relational discipleship." I couldn't agree more.

Mentoring doesn't have to be formal, either. Thank goodness we don't have to be professionals at this! Mentoring can be as simple as what Proverbs 11:25 says: "Whoever refreshes others will be refreshed." I love that. When we pour into another person, it's like we're giving her a cup of water. The surprising gift is that we get a cup of water in return.

Every time we speak God's truth to our mentee, we're reminding ourselves of its power. Every time we remind our mentee of God's promises, we bring those promises back into the forefront of our minds. And every time our mentee is blessed by the Holy Spirit during one of our mentoring sessions, we are blessed as well.

Maybe that's part of the purpose of God calling us to be mentors. He knows the double benefit it has. Our mentees benefit from the experiences of our lives; we benefit from a new understanding of present-day circumstances. Two in one. God is so good.

"Do we care enough for the next generation to share what we've learned? Will you join me in accepting this challenge? You are needed."

We can't underestimate the value of well-earned, life-long experience and wisdom. To the women of my generation and those ahead of me: you have more to offer than you realize. Do we care enough for the next generation to share what we've learned? Will you join me in accepting this challenge? You are needed.

PART 2

BE

CHAPTER 5

Be Yourself

A few years ago, a group of friends were eating lunch together when an idea popped up around the table. The women had been praying together for some time, and this was something new. One of the gals brought up the idea of ministering to younger women. The idea took off from there.

They connected with MORE Mentoring to learn about how to get a mentoring process in place. Val became their mentor coordinator, and then she became one of their first mentors. Val wasn't fully prepared for the mentee she would connect with, and at first she wasn't sure she could meet her new mentee's needs. She was relieved when her mentee didn't ask for advice. She could just listen, pray, and grow in faith right alongside her mentee—and that was enough! It became a beautiful friendship.

Val's second mentee was an immigrant—Marina from Bulgaria. Marina had a hard time meeting people in her new church community. She didn't have many close friends in the area, and felt very alone, facing various challenges in her life. Then she heard about mentoring through someone involved in the women's ministry at her church, "and it sounded amazing!" she said.

Val connected with Marina and they started their mentoring relationship. "We'd never met before so we were both a little hesitant the first couple meetings," Val recalls. "I wondered if we would connect well and whether I had something to contribute to add value to Marina's life."

Those concerns subsided soon after the two began meeting. Their relationship blossomed through their rich times spent in prayer. Marina attributes much growth and progress in her self-confidence and faith to Val's encouragement and influence. Marina is passionate to help others heal and grow in faith. She recently graduated with a Master's Degree in Counseling. She is now a mentor for others. Marina comments, "If it wasn't for the encouragement and belief Val had in me, I would have remained stuck in self-doubt. Her belief and faithful prayers for me gave me wings."

Val recognizes that God has been doing the work. "What I love about mentoring is that it's a front row seat to what God is doing in the life of my mentee. It's changing my life because I'm seeing what God is doing in Marina and how He answers our prayers!"

Val has experienced what all mentors will experience. We learn that we don't need to be perfect; we just need to be present.

Be. It's such a short word but packed with so much meaning—exist, live, arise. My favorite use of the word "be" is this: *Be* who God made *you* to *be*. You are a beautiful masterpiece, handiwork, and workmanship whom God has created for His purposes.

Do you believe that? Or do you look at yourself and, instead of seeing a beautiful masterpiece, you see a so-so piece of work? I must admit that happens to me at times. Especially as women, we tend to get down on ourselves too easily. Sadly, if our identity is wrong, we hold ourselves back from being all God calls us to be.

> **"Be who God made you to be. You are a beautiful masterpiece, handiwork, and workmanship whom God has created for His purposes."**

If we constantly think self-destructive thoughts like, *I'm not enough; my life is too messed up to be used by God; my story is full of too many mistakes; I'm not really needed; I could never have an impact*—our lives will move in that direction. We will shrink back. We won't step out in faith. We will let feelings of fear and insecurity rule rather than thoughts of boldness, courage, and confidence. We will trust more in the lack of who we are rather than in the fullness of who God is.

As women, we tend to compare ourselves to others. We can't seem to help ourselves, can we? When our comparisons reveal us coming up short, we feel pressure to be someone different, even though that's not possible. So we hide. We put

> "In the privacy of our minds, we wait for others to reach out."

walls up; we protect ourselves from being vulnerable. In the privacy of our minds, we wait for others to reach out. *Inferior women like us don't take initiative,* we tell ourselves. Oh, the complicated and hurtful web of comparison.

How many of us have deemed ourselves "less than" that vivacious leader on stage or the gifted Bible teacher and concluded, *I'm not a strong enough person or a good enough Christian to be a mentor. I'm not like [fill in the blank]. I can't be like her.*

That's right—you can't! None of us can. We can only be like *ourselves,* in the way God intended. He created each of us individually and thoughtfully. Some of us are extroverts, others are introverts. Some of us have seemingly limitless energy, while others require daily naps (I fall into the nap category). We are intellects, homebodies, entrepreneurs, artists, organizers, thinkers, worker bees—each of us has a reason for being. Our mentees will come with all kinds of personalities and quirks. And as mentors, so do we! As God weaves His beautiful masterpiece together, He knows who on earth will need each other.

For we are God's handiwork, created in Christ Jesus to do good works, which God prepared in advance for us to do (Ephesians 2:10).

Throughout Scripture, we're given lots of descriptions and roles: God's workmanship (Ephesians 2:10), vessels (Jeremiah 18:4), utensils (2 Timothy 2:21), seed planters (Matthew 13:23), burden bearers (Galatians 6:2), models (Titus 2:7-8), teachers, and trainers (Titus 2:3-5). And my personal favorite—commenders and declarers: *One generation shall commend your works to another, and shall declare your mighty acts* (Psalm 145:4, ESV). These are all roles a mentor fills, and the best part is that Jesus promises He will be with us always (Matthew 28:20). He never gives us a role to fill without being there with us.

His divine power has given us everything we need for a godly life through our knowledge of him who called us by his own glory and goodness (2 Peter 1:3).

So I want to encourage you today with these words: "You have what it takes. You already have everything you need."

- As a Christian, you have a **relationship with God**. This is the key to everything we do. (If you don't have a relationship with God, see the Appendix "Knowing the Greatest Mentor.")

> **"You have what it takes. You already have everything you need."**

- You have the **Word of God**, which is living and active. God speaks to you through His Word and tells you the things you need to know.

- You have **your story**, all uniquely yours. No one else's story is your story. And it matters. It's the culmination of your experiences. Your upbringing. Your marriage. Your labor and delivery story. Your singleness. Your infertility. Your successes. Your failures. Your imperfections. God uses our struggles and mistakes to encourage our mentees. That kind of openness brings authenticity, making us real. Your story is powerful, and it's been written for you to share with others.

- You have **spiritual gifts**. They were supernaturally given specifically to you at the moment you asked Jesus to be the Lord and Savior of your life. Spiritual gifts are to be used for Kingdom purposes and to build up the body of Christ.

- You have a **personality** that is all your own. God formed you and knit you together perfectly. Some of us are sassy and boisterous; some are empathetic and introspective—just the way we're supposed to be.

Every mentoring relationship is going to look unique. The way I mentor may be very different from the way you mentor—and that's OK!

Just *be you* and let God do the rest.

As mentors, we don't need another to-do list. We've been there, done that. We also don't need to have all the answers and live a perfect life.

What we need is a shift in attitude—from "Do-Attitudes" to "Be-Attitudes."

Consider these Be-Attitudes of a Mentor:

- Be prayerful.

- Be available.

- Be flexible.

- Be interested.

- Be real.

- Be an encourager.

- Be a listener.

- Be trustworthy.

- Be present.

Be who God made *you* to be and be there for others. Be free from trying to figure out how it will all work out. Be yourself and allow God to use you in a way no one else could.

CHAPTER 6

Be Filled

At a retreat in the mountains of Colorado many years ago, we were instructed to walk outside during one of our breaks and identify one thing that shows the glory of God. I could have quickly chosen the majestic mountains, the tall evergreen trees, or the beautiful stream, but as I sat there praying and asking God to show me His glory, I looked down and spotted a tiny drop of dew on one small blade of grass. The sun was hitting the drop just right to make a brilliant, blinding array of breathtaking colors.

That moment was such an eye-opener for me. The tiny drop simply reflected the sun, letting the beauty of the majestic rays sparkle right through it. I want to be like that little drop and simply reflect the beauty of Jesus.

I knew someone like that once.

Her name is Karen Zummo and she passed away on November 4, 2019. I had only known Karen for one year as we served on the mentoring team and prayer team at our church, but in that short time she inspired me and many others. Karen was one of those natural mentors—like a magnet that women are drawn to, someone who points them to Jesus. And Karen did just that.

Karen was fully present and compassionate. When you spent time with her you felt like you were the most important person to her in that moment. She listened so well and selflessly cared more about what you were going through than what she was going through. One Sunday as we both stood at the front of the church to pray over others, I glanced over at Karen to see her cupping her loving hands around another woman's face, looking straight into her eyes, and speaking words of truth over her. She tenderly loved people with a passion.

"She was so filled up with Jesus that He naturally flowed out of her."

Karen didn't have to strive to be a mentor. She was so filled up with Jesus that He naturally flowed out of her. We wanted to be around her because we wanted to be around Jesus. Speaking words of life came easily to Karen because she knew God's Word and she knew her God. She often encouraged many of us by just reminding us of His faithfulness and goodness.

I believe Karen had a deeper walk with God than most because she had walked a road of suffering like most of us haven't experienced. Suffering didn't make her bitter or resentful but made her more in love with Jesus.

I loved to listen to Karen pray. She had an intimacy with her Savior that was beautiful to witness. On our Monday night prayer nights, she would often stand gazing out the window just worshiping God without a thought of anyone else in the room. Karen reflected the beauty of Jesus just like that sparkling dew drop in the mountains.

This is the last verse I texted to Karen:

Do not, therefore, fling away your [fearless] confidence, for it has a glorious and great reward. For you have need of patient endurance [to bear up under difficult circumstances without compromising], so that when you have carried out the will of God, you may receive and enjoy to the full what is promised (Hebrews 10:35-36, AMP).

Karen has received her great reward! She is in heaven, enjoying to the full what God has promised her. Fullness of life.

If you're like me, you are probably thinking, *If being a mentor means I'll be expected to inspire other people like that, then I'm running the other way. Let's face it, I'm not very inspirational.* I understand. I really do. I often tell people I'm kind of a boring person; not much inspiration sparkles from me on my own.

Some days we may feel like the only thing we can do is drip, unable to even stay on the top side of the leaf to catch God's sunshine. Maybe you've mentored before and it didn't go that great. Or mentoring hasn't been as easy as you thought it might be. Perhaps more challenges than successes. We can

"WE CAN ALL FEEL LIKE WE'RE NOT DOING ENOUGH OR WE'RE SAYING THE WRONG THINGS."

all feel like we're not doing enough or we're saying the wrong things. The ideas we have fall flat. Our strength doesn't hold up. Our wisdom doesn't go far. We maybe haven't seen much transformation in our mentee. The guilt can set in.

Let's take a closer look at the word *inspire*. It is derived from "in spirit." That means if we are filled up with the Holy Spirit, then we can't help but be inspiring. What a relief! We must remember it's God's power at work within us and He sees success differently than we might.

In fact, I'd summarize God's definition of success like this: Fill up. Pour out.

Filling you up to pour into others is what MORE Mentoring is all about and it happens through the filling of the Holy Spirit. Thankfully, it's not up to us to force inspiration. It's up to God who lives in us to let it flow out of our lives.

In one sentence, this would be the goal of mentoring: *And to know this love that surpasses knowledge—that you may be filled to the measure of all the fullness of God* (Ephesians 3:19). Wow! Aside from heaven, it's hard to even fathom what that kind of life would look like. Fullness of God means fullness of life, fullness of power, and fullness of freedom, peace, and joy. I want to live that kind of life, don't you?

I have come that they may have life, and have it to the full (John 10:10).

There is something about the word "full" that intrigues me. It speaks of wholeness, reaching maturity, more than enough.

It's the opposite of emptiness or incomplete, which so many are living out today and can't seem to overcome. Is that truly what Jesus came to offer us? No! He came to offer us life, and not only life—but life to the full.

Fullness of life doesn't come from an easy life. We can go through really, really hard stuff and still live out fullness. We do that by dwelling with Him, abiding with Him. By choosing a life that's emptied of ourselves and full of God. That's where we find the rest, confidence, joy, peace, and hope that He came to give us. You know what I call that? A *personal revival*. An awakening and rebirth in our souls, a renewed refreshing in our hearts. Doesn't that sound so appealing? A personal revival within us will rejuvenate our faith, stimulate new growth, and ignite our passion for God's greater purpose in our lives. As we spend time with God, filling ourselves with His presence and power, letting His life pour into our lives, there will be a natural overflow into the lives of others around us. Our entire image of mentoring fits this idea—from our fullness in Jesus we pour into the lives of others.

The key is to focus on God and what He has done and will continue to do—not on all the things we don't do well or don't do enough of—to dwell on God's presence within us rather than the results of our efforts. When we try in our own strength, we fail. In our own failure, we reinforce the shame. No sparkly dewdrop there.

On one of my morning walks along the river near our home not long ago, I was reflecting on my Scripture reading from that morning. As I pondered on Psalm 121 and the fact that God is our maker, it suddenly dawned on me. Yes! God is the maker. He is the source of mentoring made real. He makes it real through His promises that are real. Be filled with the power of these five promises that God will pour into us as we seek Him.

Five Promises Poured into Us by God

Power

His power works within us. When we are weak, He is strong (Ephesians 3:20, 2 Corinthians 12:9).

Purpose

He will accomplish His purpose through us. His purpose might be completely different than our purpose. His ways are so much higher than ours (Isaiah 55:9, Jeremiah 29:11, Ephesians 2:10).

Presence

He will be with us and that's the best promise we can have (Joshua 1:9, Isaiah 7:14).

Peace

We can have great peace in knowing the inspiration that comes through mentoring isn't about us (Isaiah 26:3, John 14:27).

Provision

He will provide just what is needed, whether it's an

encouraging word, an answer to prayer, or time to give
(Matthew 6:33, Philippians 4:19).

If you look at the first letter in promise and the second
letter in each of the other words— Promise, power, purpose,
presence, peace, provision, you see the word "**Pourer.**" (I'm not
even sure that's a word but it was kind of cool for me when I
realized the flow of these words.) God is the divine **Pourer!** His
promises, power, purpose, presence, peace, and provision start
with Him and come through Him. We just let Him pour into
our lives, our soul and spirit, and keep on pouring through us.

How do we go about being filled with God? Through
reading God's Word and prayer. So simple and yet so powerful
and so transforming. Every day, I
run to God's Word, and I spend
time with God in prayer. I want to
show others why my life isn't falling
apart. It's because my Bible is falling
apart. This is my relationship with
God.

> "*God is the divine
> Pourer! His
> promises, power,
> purpose, presence,
> peace, and provision
> start with Him and
> come through Him.*"

I leave my Bible open throughout my day and when I have conver-
sations with others, I can say, "My Bible is open to this passage;
here's what I read this morning and I pray it will encourage
you." It always amazes me how God ministers to someone else
after I fill up with Him and just simply pour Him out.

What is the role of a mentor again? We simply fill up with
Jesus and pour Him out to others. That pretty much says it all.

Those lives are supernaturally impacted through the divine work of the Holy Spirit through us. How do we continue to stay filled? We come running to Jesus each day, emptying ourselves and asking Him to fill us up. He is the Living Water. He is the River of Life. He is the Overflow in our lives when we are filled with Him.

What would it look like if we as the Church all said, "I will fill up with Jesus and pour Him out to whomever He puts in my path?" I expect there would be some major spikes in church attendance as people become inspired to experience more.

People want the Jesus in you. Not more advice, opinions, or information. Stay in God's Word. Stay close to Him in prayer. Stay filled up. Inspiration will flow.

> "*People want the Jesus in you.*"

Deeper Trust

Being filled doesn't mean we won't suffer. It means we go deeper in trust. Pregnant at 15 weeks, Madalyn lay in the hospital bed, unable to prevent her body from going into early delivery. A premature rupture had resulted in the loss of all her amniotic fluid. The baby was coming way too early and nothing could be done to save it. She phoned her mentor, knowing she would pray, and pray fervently.

The baby did not survive, and Madalyn returned home with a broken heart and damaged trust. As the days went on, she could hardly lift her hands to pray. She was in such grief she could do little more than cry at Jesus's feet.

A few weeks later, Madalyn and her mentor went for a walk, and Madalyn started asking the inevitable hard questions.

"How could a good God let something like this happen? Why? What purpose could there be in all this? How can I go on?" She sobbed on a park bench in her neighborhood, processing through the devastation of losing her baby.

Her mentor sat with Madalyn in her pain. Although her mentor had more life experience, she couldn't answer all of Madalyn's heartbroken questions. Who could? She did, however, validate the wounded mother's feelings with phrases like "I'm sad with you. I've never been through what you're going through, but I know it hurts terribly." The mentor listened, cried with Madalyn, and prayed with her for comfort and for God to restore her faith, even amid such excruciating loss.

The two women continued working through the *Together* mentoring guide over the next few months. Through their prayer times together, they poured their hearts out to God and learned more about who God is, the fullness of life He desires for us, and even about His purpose in the pain.

Gently, Madalyn's mentor reminded her, over and over, that God does see her. He does see her pain. He is right there walking with her as she stumbles through hard days and harder questions—is God really trustworthy? Is He really good? Really?

Madalyn reached a pivotal point of either turning towards God or turning away from God. Thankfully, Madalyn chose to stand on the truths of who God is: a loving Father who hurts when we hurt. Who walks beside us in our doubt. And who desires an abundant full life for us, despite—and amidst—the pain.

A year later, Madalyn admits she has more clarity and peace in having struggled. By confessing those hard questions and processing them out loud with her mentor, her trust is on the road to healing. Plus, Madalyn's story has a happy ending.

Madalyn writes:

"As I sit here writing this, I am holding my 6-week-old daughter. Daily, I am in complete awe of how we got here. Her life represents so much redemption for our family. If it had all worked out how I originally thought I wanted it to, she wouldn't be here. But she is. God must have a big purpose for her life. I trust that He does.

"If there's one thing I can tell you it's that God is faithful. He has been faithful to me and He is and will be faithful to you. This isn't the path I would have chosen. But looking back I can tell you, I wouldn't change it.

> **"If there's one thing I can tell you it's that God is faithful. He has been faithful to me and He is and will be faithful to you."**

Because of such dark days I know Jesus like I never have before, and having a mentor to walk with me through that has been a huge part of my story."

If we're being real, let's admit—real life threatens real trust. We come into the world bright-eyed and hopeful, then life hits. Our faith in God gets shaken when bad things happen. People let us down. In truth, we even lose trust in ourselves, terrified we'll repeat past mistakes. Negative past experiences, within the church or due to our own faults, haunt us with distrust in our own spiritual life. When you add to this the mentee's hurts (many by Christians) and a modern-day culture that ridicules believing in Jesus, well, that's a lot. We pray, we believe, and still things go in the wrong direction. What does this do to our trust?

When my friend Karen Zummo died, after months of praying fervently for her healing, I confess I wrestled with my disappointment in God. We had stood in her hospital room, mature Christians united and confident for a divine miracle, and yet she died. That hurt. I couldn't force myself to go back to prayer nights. All I could think of was Karen standing there every week praising Jesus. Even being at church was hard.

Eventually I reached a place of acceptance. In the middle of my pain, I returned my whole heart and trust to God. But it didn't happen immediately. It took time. Even though He didn't answer our prayers for Karen the way we'd wanted, I determined I would rather live my life trusting in God's love for us, in His Holy nature, than in the hopeless despair I see in the world every day.

I share this story because I suspect many of you have similar stories. Dear friends confide in me their sorrow over seemingly unanswered prayers. Healing doesn't happen. Adult children wander. Relationships don't improve. After praying for years without seeing any changes, discouragement sets in. That's so understandable. That kind of real pain has the potential to destroy real trust in God. And that's right where the enemy wants to keep us, buried in doubt and distrust.

Would it surprise you to hear that Jesus Himself tells us we can't muster up enough faith to trust God on our own? When the disciples ask Him, basically, "How in the world can anyone be saved?" Jesus answers, *"With man this is impossible, but with God all things are possible"* (Matthew 19:26).

> **"He is as trustworthy today as He was the day He breathed life into all of creation."**

Be encouraged! None of this is a surprise to God. He formed the foundations of the earth, and He is the same yesterday, today, and forever. He is as trustworthy today as He was the day He breathed life into all of creation.

The Bible warns us of opposition. In I John 4:3 we read, *. . . but every spirit that does not acknowledge Jesus is not from God. This is the spirit of the antichrist, which you have heard is coming and even now is already in the world.* No kidding. We see evidence of this evil anti-Jesus spirit all over the world.

So, yes, our trust in God meets opposition, over and over again, throughout our lives. That's the world we live in. We will face failure, doubts, fears, unmet expectations. Thankfully, we have the power within us to replace those lies with God's truth:

> *You, dear children, are from God and have overcome them, because the ONE who is in you is greater than the one who is in the world* (I John 4:4, emphasis mine).

Here's where the victory comes, dear ones. We pray and we surrender the outcome to our capable, loving Father. We don't understand the course, but we trust in God's character, His goodness. We live out our trust in God, even in the thick of a story we wouldn't have written ourselves. If we were writing our own story, we would never allow tragedy, disappointment, or death. We would all celebrate peaceful lives with happy endings. But that isn't real life.

Time and again (and we all know it's true), suffering leads us to a closer place with God—*if* we turn *to* Him rather than *away from* Him. During those distressing trials, we experience His mercy and His love more intimately. Those are tender, precious times and they build our faith.

> *Time and again (and we all know it's true), suffering leads us to a closer place with God—if we turn to Him rather than away from Him.*

I was so sad when my friend Karen died. I asked God a lot of questions. All the while, He patiently listened and held me close, understanding my grief. When my disappointment calmed and I chose to renew my trust in God, I experienced His gentle presence and His complete acceptance with no hint of condemnation or rejection.

From that place of intimacy with Jesus, I now have even more empathy for the women God brings into my life to mentor. I can honestly say, "I feel your pain," and offer sincere comfort that comes from a shared battle. I can relate to the inner conflict and declare, "There is hope!" Through the combat and drudgery of real life, we can place our real trust in a real God and His real promises. Why would we turn anywhere else?

CHAPTER 7

Real Relationships

Peggy had seen Merry Jo at a mentoring gathering and felt like she might be the type of person she could connect well with. As Peggy reached out, Merry Jo responded with a resounding "Yes!" As their mentoring relationship developed, their conversations started to include the topic of race and racial inequities centering on Peggy's experiences as a black woman. The backdrop of their conversation was the civil unrest about race taking place around the country. During an interview with MORE Mentoring, Peggy and Merry Jo (who is white), shared openly about their journey specific to that dynamic in mentor/mentee relationships.

Peggy's calm words of personal experience and godly wisdom are a challenge to white Christians everywhere: "Racial injustice is a big part of my life. I can get in my car to go to the store tomorrow and not get back. That's a reality for me. For me to talk about that in a mentor/mentee relationship requires trust. A lot of times the attitudes and languages in churches, the response, when we bring up these kinds of discussions, has not been kind. As Christians we are called to be uncomfortable. Our faith calls us to sometimes step out of our comfort zones and trust God. So taking steps to mentor someone of a different race or ethnicity, which I can speak to because I am a black woman, and allowing God to build that authenticity is really a greater declaration of love. We don't do it from a 'savior' perspective: 'I'm here to save this poor black girl who must be going through this bad stuff,' or just from a myopic point of view, but to understand a black or brown sister in the church. How can I come alongside her and love her, truly love her as being created in the image of the Lord? What does that mean for her? Like I said, it's not a comfortable discussion to have but I believe the Lord is pushing us in that direction to really love each other authentically."

Peggy said that beautifully and I want to shout it to the world!

We can do this better. We can meet with other people who don't look the same as we do, who don't believe the same as we do. What unity we could achieve if more of us reached out and loved each other well, regardless of our skin color or anything else that causes division within us.

Peggy values Merry Jo's sincere listening, to her and to the Holy Spirit. As sisters in Christ, the love they have for each other is undeniable. They exemplify bridging our differences in relationship.

Relationship is a scary word. We oftentimes don't know how to start or develop a relationship, and the uncertainties of what to expect can be paralyzing. Especially when we consider an unknown relationship with someone unlike us—different race, generation, status, or whatever other obstacle creates an invisible barrier between us.

> "*We oftentimes don't know how to start or develop a relationship, and the uncertainties of what to expect can be paralyzing.*"

It breaks my heart that we are so divided in our country. I cringe when I hear reports of hate crimes, or overhear demeaning words spoken toward others who are different, words that make people feel small or less than, words that tear down rather than build up.

That's not God's way.

It's time for God's people to have honest, mutually respectful conversations about diversity and racial reconciliation, about generational differences, about differences of all kinds. God's heart is for all His people to live in real relationships, mutually appreciative of one another.

How good and pleasant it is when God's people live together in unity! (Psalm 133:1).

Can you imagine? What if we had real and honest conversations—both talking and listening—about the dividing issues that are so real between us? What if we truly had empathy for one another and tried to understand what it feels like to walk in each other's shoes? Our hearts would be softened. We wouldn't lash out so quickly. We would be changed.

God, bring us together so we can glorify You and receive Your blessing.

Here's a challenge for you. Seek out a mentor or a mentee who is not like you. Who has a different skin color or who is much older or younger? Who comes from a different culture? Who maybe even speaks a different language? Try Google translate as you converse! (Keep in mind that MORE Mentoring already has guides #1, 2, and 3 translated into Spanish, and other languages are targeted for translation in the future.)

Once you invite that person into a relationship, really listen to her. I mean, lean in and intentionally seek to understand. Don't get defensive. Don't try to explain your way of thinking. But really listen to learn. To get her.

I love those three short words that make up the word "together." *To—get—her*. A mentoring relationship begins first with a pursuit. We pursue a mentee. We go after her "to get her." Sometimes a mentee will pursue the mentor. We all want to be pursued, to be wanted. Then the relationship moves forward in sincerely getting to know each other. The mentor takes the lead by asking questions to help get to know the mentee, taking the time to listen, to understand, *to get her*. Every woman wants to be seen. To be heard. To be known. And as mentor and mentee work *together*, they will begin to understand each other better.

"HERE'S A CHALLENGE FOR YOU. SEEK OUT A MENTOR OR A MENTEE WHO IS NOT LIKE YOU."

To—get—her, together.

When I was a young mom, I promised the Lord I would never forget how grueling it was to be a mom. I loved it, but it sure wasn't easy. Those years were beyond question the most difficult time in my marriage, in my walk with the Lord, in my feelings of inadequacy as a mother.

I would have loved a mentor who invested in me. I believe it would have made such a huge difference in my life. To have a woman who is a little further down the path show love and acceptance—without judgment or comparison—is huge. And then to have her pray regarding specific things is absolutely life-changing. I've seen it firsthand, and I've heard those words come out of the mouths of moms who have had mentors like that.

As my kids have grown, I have made another promise to the Lord: that if He wants to use me to mentor others, I'm available and willing. If He promises to be with me, I'm all in. I hope you'll join me.

Four Pillars of Mentoring

So how do we go about developing real relationships? How do we make mentoring simple yet powerful? Through my mentoring relationships with other women, I've learned the bottom line is this: Keep it simple! I have found four key words to be vital in every mentoring relationship. I call them the four pillars of mentoring:

1. Love

2. Listen

3. Encourage

4. Pray

Let's look together at these simple, yet powerful, four pillars of mentoring,

Pillar #1 is LOVE.

The goal of a mentor is for her mentee to experience more of Jesus, to be filled to the measure of all the fullness of God, to know His love. We begin that process by demonstrating the love of God ourselves. When I think

> "As mentors, we each have the opportunity to influence the lives of others, simply by showing them the love of Jesus."

of a woman whose heart is filled with more love than anyone else on earth, I picture a mother loving her child. A mother's love is powerful, relentless, effective, and nurturing. Sometimes mentors are called "spiritual mothers." They don't carry all the responsibilities of a real mom, of course, but they can be a loving influence with a mother's kind of heart. And we all need them.

I'm so thankful that I've been blessed with many spiritual mothers in my lifetime. They have shaped my view of God and His power. Their examples of living out the love of Jesus have changed my life. As mentors, we each have the opportunity to influence the lives of others, simply by showing them the love of Jesus.

Here are some practical ways we mentors can show love to our mentees:

Make time for her. Be flexible. Consistency and structure do not always happen in a younger woman's life. Keep your options open. Make yourself available when you can. The gift of your time can be the greatest gift given. The gift of uninterrupted time speaks volumes. Set aside time to devote completely to your mentee. Let her know she is so important, so loved that you have set everything else aside for her.

Ask good questions. Especially ones that start with why. Be interested. Ask about her everyday life. Follow up your first question with a second question. Can you elaborate on that? How did that make you feel? Absorb her answers instead of thinking about the next question.

Seek to understand her feelings. Our feelings are not always logical or factual. However, they do have extreme value. Our feelings serve as signals to deeper concerns. Sometimes we need to work through layers of feelings to get to the core of what is causing them. One of my young mentees showed me a new way to look at the word intimacy. She called it "in to me see." For sure, we can do that! Keep in mind, not all mentees will be willing to open up to this level of intimacy, and that's OK too. We only go as deep as she wants.

Care about what she cares about. Step into her world. Consider the demands on her life. Put yourself in her shoes. Show empathy. Feel what she is feeling. Validate her feelings.

Express interest in those matters that are important to her.

Support her unconditionally. This will require God's unconditional love flowing from within you. A woman will sense if she is being judged or tolerated. Ask God to help you support your mentee throughout your time together. If your mentee feels like you will love her no matter what she shares with you, if you accept her just as she is, you are creating a safe environment for going deeper. She is longing for authenticity and it will be so encouraging for her to have someone she can be open and real with.

Take action. Sometimes love is best expressed through action. Watch your mentee's kids for her so she can have a break or deliver a home-cooked meal to your homesick mentee's college dorm. Acts of love often outweigh words.

Pillar #2 is LISTEN.

Guess what the Bible has to say about listening? A lot.

Everyone should be quick to listen, slow to speak and slow to become angry (James 1:19b).

Therefore consider carefully how you listen (Luke 8:18a).

Let the wise listen and add to their learning (Proverbs 1:5a).

To answer before listening—that is folly and shame (Proverbs 18:13).

Mentors who are good listeners will have tremendous

influence because their mentees will leave each session feeling known, validated, understood, loved, affirmed, valued, and respected.

How can we listen well to our mentees?

Listen more than you talk. We can't listen if we're talking. I would say over 50% of mentoring is listening. My own style is about 80% listening. People are craving someone they can talk to, someone who will listen. I would much rather listen than talk—that's just me. But it is also biblical. *Be quick to listen. Slow to speak.* Spend more time listening than talking. We all have a need to be heard. We all need someone in our lives we can share our biggest secrets with who won't interrupt us, who sincerely listens.

Be fully present. No distractions. Other people can tell when we are not fully engaged or thinking about other things. Look her in the eyes. Be present. Show her you really care by being all there. It's better to be a mentor who is present rather than one who tries to be perfect.

Listen to her heart. Your mentee will feel so cared for and valued when she is heard. Consider her tone and watch her body language at the same time. Pray for discernment to determine what is going on inside of her. Listen past shallow answers.

Listen to remember. Pay attention to her answers. Remember to follow up on the important (or not so important) things she shares with you.

Don't be a fixer. This means sitting with her in the pit with

"LISTEN MORE THAN YOU TALK."

no "fixes" on the agenda. Don't try to solve each problem she shares. She's often not looking for an answer. She wants to process with someone. She wants to be heard.

I can often be heard saying to my dear husband, "I don't need a fixer-upper right now. I need empathy." Bless his heart. He loves to fix and make things better because he wants the best for me. But what I need most is what all of us need most: someone to listen as we process and share the deeper things in our heart.

Repeat back to her. Take the time and effort to clarify what she has shared with you. Repeat it back to her to make sure you have heard it correctly.

Write it down. Take notes if you need to. I take notes often. That way, I'm hearing her but I'm also seeing it on paper. It helps me to remember.

Pillar #3 is ENCOURAGE.

I'm realizing more and more that encouraging others doesn't come naturally to everyone. Most likely, you have some people in your life who aren't very good at encouraging. They aren't trying to be discouraging. It's almost as if they just don't realize how their words can come across as hurtful or critical. Their silence can even be discouraging because it seems like they don't care.

In contrast, do you have anyone in your life who is superb at encouraging and almost every word out of her mouth builds up and doesn't tear down? I do. Those people really stand out and I'm drawn to them and want to be around them. I want to be that kind of a person.

Encouragement is a spiritual gift. Even though we may not have the gift, each of us can still grow in becoming better encouragers.

"Quite literally, when we encourage someone, we are putting courage within them."

The definition of encouragement is to give support, confidence, or hope to someone. Quite literally, when we *encourage* someone, we are putting *courage* within them. I find that fascinating and hopeful!

Hebrews 10:25 says, . . . *let us encourage one another with words of hope* (NIRV).

Encouraging one another with words of hope is one of the most important things we can do as mentors. Make people feel better than how you found them.

Here are some practical ways to encourage others:

Notice the good and speak it. Notice it in your mentee, in her kids, in her husband, in her situation. As we love and listen first, be aware of the good that you can bring out in what she is going through. Speak it to her and over her. She needs hope, to be reminded of the good that can come from bad situations. A simple word of encouragement to remind her she's doing OK will go a long way.

Stay positive. Don't get pulled down into negativity. She might be sharing some discouraging things and you can certainly empathize with her and seek to understand her, but always try to stay positive and speak positively.

Speak truth over her. Read or quote Scripture that applies to her situation. Uplift her with promises from God's Word. When you share a verse with someone, the Holy Spirit can take it from there and use it in such powerful and personal ways. One time my mentor shared a verse with me that I had just read that morning. It was such a confirmation and I knew it was directly from the Lord. Also, speak the truth in love. Sometimes that means speaking the hard things. It may not feel encouraging at the time, but God can use the truth to bring encouragement in the future as well. There are times to be silent and there are times to quote Scripture. Try to be sensitive enough to the Spirit to know the difference between the two.

Share your story. There is power in your story, no matter how dull or traumatic. Embrace your own story and share it bravely. Share what has been tough or discouraging or even not what you expected. Share the challenging things you have gone through, how you have botched things up. This shows your mentee she is not alone. So often we feel like we are the only ones struggling or feeling like a failure. Hearing how others have also dealt with these feelings helps tremendously. (Note of caution: Only share the intimacies of your story with your mentee if she is ready to hear it. If she isn't mature or healthy enough to handle certain parts of your story, wait until she's ready. If she doesn't ever get there, that's OK too. Ask the Holy Spirit to show you how much to share.)

Build trust. We build trust by being authentic. A mentee will more likely trust a mentor who is real. As mentors, we offer tremendous encouragement when we share openly and honestly. Don't be afraid to share your weaknesses. Our mentees want to hear how we deal with our problems and what God has taught us because of them. Be real. Authenticity is what women are looking for, not another authority. They want to hear how you have messed up. What would you do differently? What have you learned from your mistakes?

Assure her you are a safe place for her to share her own troubles. Promise confidentiality and no judgment. Confidentiality is so important to developing trust. When she confides in you, keep your promise. Prove to her that anything she shares with you will stay with you.

Share your current journey with her. She will love hearing what you are going through—the good, the hard, the easy, the challenges.

> *"If you've never prayed out loud before, give yourself grace and give yourself space to try it."*

Pillar #4 is PRAY.

When I have asked mentees how they best felt encouraged by a mentor, they have brought up prayer—and not just her mentor promising she would be praying for her, but praying with her right at that moment. Praying with and over our mentees makes them feel so loved and cared for, and our prayers model effective praying for them. We show her how to go to God with every concern that is on her heart.

You may have a lot of experience with prayer or maybe very little. No worries. If you've never prayed out loud before, give yourself grace and give yourself space to try it. You will get more comfortable the more you just do it.

Early in my journey of praying with others, during our silent confession time I would concentrate on not swallowing because it sounded so loud in my ears. The more I concentrated, the more I had to swallow. I was so self-conscious! And one time someone looked up from our prayer time together and asked, "Did you know that your nose makes a squeaking noise when you breathe?" *Oh my!*

I just have to laugh because I know God loves it when I come to Him so imperfectly, big swallows and squeaky nose and all my other shortcomings. He knows we're imperfect creatures. He just wants us to come to Him in prayer, squeaks included.

So these are the four Pillars of Mentoring: Love, Listen, Encourage, Pray. If you model these four pillars, I know God will use your life to greatly impact others.

CHAPTER 8

Real Prayer

At a meeting for young moms a few years ago, I sat listening to one of the mothers as she expressed concern over her son. He was experiencing high anxiety and she didn't know what to do. Before I could suggest we pray, another mom piped up with, "Essential oils!"

I turned to her in surprise.

"That's what your little boy needs!" she insisted. "Just rub (such and such) oil on his inner arm before he goes to school, and he'll be fine. You'll see." Other moms nodded in agreement and the conversation shifted to some other less urgent topic.

As the chatter resumed, I remained silent. And disappointed. I have nothing against essential oils, and they may very well have been the right solution. But shouldn't we have asked Jesus for His counsel? He is the One who knows best, always.

This is a common occurrence among women. We love to give advice, and quite frankly, we have lots of valuable advice to give. We're the queens of advice columns. Think of all the limitless hosts of bloggers and podcasters. But truthfully, we don't always know what's best, even though we might think we do.

As mentors, we can actually do a damaging disservice to our mentees if we rely on our own know-it-all textbook of advice instead of thinking to pray first. We might incorrectly advise, for example, "Yes, you should look for a different job," when God's plan is to strengthen her character through the conflict in her workplace. Or, "Of course you have a right to be mad at your husband after what he did. Vent it all out," when God wants to work on a deeply buried character flaw in the wife instead. How will we know what God's greater purpose is unless we ask Him?

I'd like to be so bold as to say this: If a wise thought chisels its way into the forefront of our mind and we believe we should share it—pray first and ask God what to share, what not to say, what to do, what not to do. We're not expected to know every answer to our mentees' probing questions, but Jesus knows. That's why we pray together. We might be amazed at how the Holy Spirit directs our dialogue. He may plant an alternative in our mind we hadn't considered. Listen for His gentle guidance.

Relying on our own expertise alone causes us to not only run the risk of giving misdirected advice, but even worse, we miss the opportunity to show how important and vital prayer

"THE BEST
ANSWER FOR
ANY CONCERN IS
FOUND THROUGH
PRAYER."

is to our lives. The best answer for any concern is found through prayer. That and so much more.

The other day I was reading in Isaiah when the words "Wonderful Counselor" jumped to my attention. Yes! Jesus is the *most* wonderful counselor. He's the One we should go to for answers, for healing, for divine activity in our lives. Through prayer, we will get to know not only a wonderful human mentor or mentee, but we will get to know the Greatest Mentor of all time. And really that includes three Mentors in One—the Father, the Son, and the Holy Spirit. It doesn't get any better than that!

That's why at MORE Mentoring we call it prayer-focused mentoring. Prayer changes our mentoring from natural to supernatural. God puts the "super" in our "natural." When we invite Him in, He shows up and does the inner healing, the miracles, the wonders, that we could never do on our own. And the exciting adventure of prayer is that He often waits until we pray before He does that kind of supernatural work.

If we don't pray, we're missing out on so much of what God has for us. Prayer is the way we get to know God better, where we learn to listen to His voice. Through prayer we begin to recognize real answers to real prayer. When we pray, we experience miracles as well as simple answers to simple prayers. And that builds real faith.

So, yes! The most important thing we can do in our mentoring relationships is to pray together. I've talked with women who are fearful of praying out loud. They expect others will judge the way they pray or don't pray. Without much experience praying out loud, they feel awkward, not sure what to say. That's so normal. Any of us feel uncomfortable when we first try something we're not familiar with. Sometimes we think of prayer as being such a personal thing that it's hard to pray out loud and share these intimate feelings and requests with other people. I encourage you to take baby steps. If you cry the whole way through the first time of praying out loud, well, that's just fine. It shows your beautiful heart. God loves your tender heart and He's drawn to it. Plus, your vulnerability might be just what another person needs to help them open up in prayer.

> **"God doesn't require fancy prayers for us to be heard. He wants our real prayers."**

Here's something to make us all feel at ease: God doesn't require fancy prayers for us to be heard. He wants our *real prayers*. The real deal, not polished or refined words of poetry. It's not in praying the most beautiful, eloquent prayer; it's about praying from your heart. You may have very little experience in praying out loud and could feel intimidated praying with someone with a lot more experience, but don't let that stop you from praying honestly.

Do I hear a collective "whew" here? Isn't it comforting to know we can pray without trying so hard? Prayer is a plain, honest conversation with God, our loving Father. He doesn't judge us as we pray. He loves to hear from us! He doesn't care as much about the words that mumble out of our mouth as much as He cares about the words of our heart—that authentic place within us. Let the words of your heart flow to the open, receiving ears of God.

To mentors and mentees alike, when it comes to praying together: Just do it! Practice. The more you pray out loud together, the more comfortable you will become. And what a difference it will make in your lives. When it comes to prayer, we are all pilgrims, not professionals. We continue to learn and grow. We are all on different journeys, so the most important thing to remember is we all have to start somewhere. None of us has matured to the point that our prayers could no longer benefit from improvement. Remember that God accepts each of us just as we are.

There is not a right or wrong way to pray, but there are ways to have prayer be more powerful and effective.

The prayer of a righteous person is powerful and effective (James 5:16b).

These four principles of prayer have been effective for many mentors and mentees.

1. Praise

2. Confession

3. Thanksgiving

4. Asking

It's natural to go to #4 first. We want answers. But if that is our main goal for prayer, we set ourselves up for disappointment when God is silent and the answer doesn't come for a while. Plus, we shortchange ourselves. Real prayer is so much more than coming before God with a list.

I had a two-year season of my life where I pleaded with God for an answer and I only heard His silence. I've also had a long season of my life where God made a promise and didn't fulfill that promise until 18 years later. Did either of those seasons mean He wasn't right there and wasn't listening? No. He was so very near, weaving something beautiful out of my life. I just needed patience and a deeper trust that He hadn't forgotten me. Both of those seasons were great seasons of growth in my life and drew me ever closer to the heart of God.

> *"To put it simply, prayer is an interactive relationship with Jesus."*

God is mysterious in His ways. We won't fully know Him until heaven. But until then, we can have a life-altering relationship with Him through prayer and His living Word. To put it simply, prayer is an interactive relationship with Jesus.

We can alleviate some of the uncertainties of how to pray together with our mentees (and on our own!) by following the four principles of prayer.

1. Praise

Begin your prayer times by looking up with a heart of praise and worship. Praise God for who He is, for His attributes and His character. We get our eyes off our circumstances and dwell on the fact that He is able to do anything. The impossible becomes possible when we acknowledge His greatness.

Together mentors and mentees can take turns praising God in their own words. Real words. No showy words necessary—just words from our heart. Using Scripture is also helpful in effective prayer. Praying the Word of God brings the will of God into our circumstances. We can read or quote Scriptures throughout all four of these prayer principles.

2. Confession

Look within with a heart of confession. Examine our hearts, uncover our sin and confess it; the only way to be filled with the Spirit is to empty ourselves of sin. To verbalize it is powerful. To admit sin to God in front of another person is humbling yet so freeing. Sin loosens its grip when it is spoken out loud and brought into the light. Confession breaks its hold on us.

3. Thanksgiving

Look around with a thankful heart. Thank God for what you see. Look behind you to see how God has been so faithful to you in the past. Look beside you at the many blessings you have right now, and then look ahead and thank God for how He will answer in His perfect way. We can't be anxious, bitter, hopeless, and thankful at the same time. Having a thankful heart changes us.

4. Asking

Look to Jesus with a heart of bold faith and ask. Picture Jesus standing before you saying, "What do you want Me to do for you?" He wants us to ask Him, even though He already knows what we need. He knows how good it is for us to come to Him and humbly ask. And He desires to answer and show us great and mighty things we would never know if we didn't ask.

Ask Him specific questions and then listen to how He answers. When I say listen, I mean be quiet. It seems kind of funny to have this be a part of our prayer time. But when we think about it, prayer is all about having a relationship with God and communicating with Him. Sometimes we need to be quiet and still and *let Him talk with us*. So if there are times of quiet in your prayer time, don't panic and think you have to fill it with talk time. Tell God you long to hear what He has to say to you and then really listen.

What do You want me to know?

What do You want me to do?

The sheep know their Shepherd's voice, the Bible says in John 10, meaning we can recognize the voice of the Holy Spirit speaking to our heart. But we have to be listening.

These four principles of effective prayer are not complicated or burdensome. Quite the opposite. Sincere praise, confession, thanksgiving, and asking will come more naturally the more we pray *real prayer.*

PART 3

MOVE

CHAPTER 9

Move Together

To be a mentor is to be an influencer. But that doesn't mean we need to recruit 10,000 followers on social media and host our own YouTube channel. We influence others without any frills by living out what we believe, and that makes people want to learn from us.

And it's easier than you might think!

Here's what a mentor is not—a mentor is not a counselor, a psychiatrist, or Bible scholar. A mentor is not an expert training an apprentice. Mentoring is not the same as what many would describe as traditional discipleship. We don't need to spend hours getting ready or work through detailed lessons every time we meet. In fact, as a mentor we don't need to work at being an influencer at all.

Instead, when we follow the MORE Mentoring model, we simply meet and share our stories (the MORE Mentoring guidebooks called *Together* provide prompts and directions to make the process a little easier), pray together, and watch God work in our lives. And the amazing thing is both of us grow closer to Him in the process. As mentor and mentee move forward together, the mentee gains more confidence in her relationship with Jesus. And that's the whole point. When our mentee wakes up at 2:00 a.m. with fear gripping her heart, we want her to know her God so well that she can turn to Him and have a conversation with Him and know His voice. It's why we do what we do.

> "One of the most unexpected blessings of mentoring is that we often experience more of Jesus when we're together."

One of the most unexpected blessings of mentoring is that we often experience more of Jesus when we're together. I'm not sure I can even explain why that is, but I've certainly experienced it in my own life. And from what many of my fellow mentors and mentees have shared, they have experienced a special presence of Jesus while praying together as well. I treasure my personal time with Jesus. In the morning, I look forward to curling up in my cozy chair by the window, my Bible in hand. Those early morning quiet times fuel my spirit and fill my heart with God's love. But there's something absolutely empowering about praying with others.

Maybe it's as simple as what Jesus taught the disciples.

"For where two or three gather in my name, there am I with them" (Matthew 18:20). Yes He is! Time and time again, mentors and mentees describe their prayer times together as powerful or filled with the Spirit. What blesses me most about that is the simplicity of praying together. It's not one person praying for the other, but both entering into prayer, seeking Jesus together.

Mutual Mentoring

My friend Barb is 10 years older than me and she calls me her mentor. I always laugh when she says that because I call her my mentor, too. I have walked with Jesus longer than she has but she has been in ministry leadership longer than I have. We learn so much from each other. We have different giftings and we call out those giftings in each other and stay teachable to learn from one another. She always points me to Jesus and my aim is to do the same for her.

Barb and I are moving forward in our individual spiritual lives together. We move together when we pray together and ask God to step into every aspect of our lives.

I think we're on to something. **"We're designed to benefit one another."** Because of the way we both pour into each other's lives, we could call our wonderful relationship nothing less than *mutual mentoring*. And that's the eventual hope for all mentoring relationships!

In God's master plan, He created each of us with an essential role to fill in the body of Christ. We're designed to benefit one another. We are all learners, and we can definitely learn from each other. As we demonstrate mentoring with the four pillars—love, listen, encourage, and pray—our mentees learn to reciprocate. They might be younger than us and maybe they haven't walked with Jesus as long as we have, but as they grow and mature, they begin to pour into our lives in return. Isn't that just like the Kingdom of God? It's backwards. It's upside down. We get filled up by pouring out. That's what mutual mentoring is all about.

Mutual interest. Mutual commitment. Mutual moving forward.

As a relationship moves forward to mutual mentoring, both parties take action. It's not always the mentee reaching out to her mentor. And it's not always the mentor pursuing the mentee. There may be occasions when one is reaching out more than the other but in general, both desire connection with the other.

I'm always honored when people reach out to me and share a concern or ask me to pray for them because they trust me and know I care. It makes me feel needed and wanted and loved. I also know there are so many times I could do more pursuing, more encouraging, more reaching out. The guilt tries to trickle in and cause me to start thinking, *I'm not doing enough. I'm not who she needs me to be.* But then I give myself grace, recognizing God's bigger picture of His plan for mentoring. The full weight doesn't fall on one person.

If a mentee sits back and waits for the other person to call or send texts to check in, if she doesn't take initiative, or even withdraws, that's not moving forward *together* because it's so one-sided. It also becomes draining when one person continues to do all the pouring out. Mutual mentoring is when both sides are invested—when both are pouring into the relationship and not sapping the strength from it.

Movement gives us hope as we draw closer to God together. Moving forward together is our mission, not dragging someone else along.

> **"Moving forward together is our mission, not dragging someone else along."**

I don't carry a burden for my friend Barb's spiritual growth, and she doesn't feel responsible for mine either. How much a mentee grows spiritually isn't the mentor's responsibility, *thank goodness*. We pour into our mentee's lives, *trusting God for the outcome*. All He calls us to do is to be willing, faithful, and consistent.

Meeting with a mentee one or two times will yield little fruit, in either the mentee or the mentor. We don't commit to mentoring a mentee a couple of times, or every once in a while, or only as long as we see positive results. Effective mentoring doesn't come through what we do occasionally; it happens through what we do consistently.

I want to help you go into mentoring with realistic expectations. Once we're willing to enter into a mentoring relationship, we can establish a limited length of time—six months, for example. Some mentors and mentees agree to work through a mentoring resource together, such as the MORE Mentoring *Together*, 12-session guide, committing to a bi-weekly meeting for 12 weeks. We can predetermine a length of time or number of get-togethers. What we can't do is rush progress.

Some mentees are prepped and ready to grow, while others require more time, and more of our patience. Those quick sprouters bring such joy early in the relationship! We feel encouraged, even successful, although we know God is responsible for the increase, not us. But there are some mentees who, for whatever reason, don't come along so easily. Those mentoring relationships don't feel as good, at least not in the beginning.

Just like a gardener drops seeds into the soil in early spring and doesn't harvest ripe produce until late summer, we might not see much progress at first. The waiting can get long. It's easy to get discouraged and doubt your ability to mentor. During those times, it's important to remind yourself that God has only called you to be obedient, and that the hard times, even in mentoring, will help *both* of you strengthen your faith.

An additional word of encouragement for those times when the connection just plain isn't going well: *It's OK.* Give yourself some grace. God never wastes a moment of pouring into someone else for His sake. We plant the seed. God makes it grow. We won't connect well with everybody. We all have different needs, styles, preferences, and personalities. You just be faithful to be who God made you to be and let Him be God.

"WE PLANT THE SEED. GOD MAKES IT GROW."

Trust Him with the connection or lack of it.

Remain faithful, dear mentor. Keep your focus on what we want *most* over what we want *now*. We want to honor God through our obedience. And we want each precious mentee to know Jesus better. We fulfill our mentoring commitment not by the harvest we reap but by the seeds we sow. So we keep on sowing seeds, one session at a time and one life at a time.

Let's be women who move together—united in purpose and growing into the fullness of who God has made us to be, each with our own unique story—in the direction of God's best plans and purposes for us. Let's move forward, toward each other and toward God, together.

CHAPTER 10

Move Beyond

I don't go to many movies, but I went to one a few years ago that made me cry. The movie is *The War Room*, and it became one of my favorites of all time. In the movie, an elderly widow decides to sell her house. When she meets the realtor, who happens to be a younger woman (played brilliantly by Priscilla Shirer), the older woman pursues a relationship with the young woman, seeing her need for a closer walk with Jesus. They don't use the word mentor in the movie, but that is exactly what is happening. The two women spend time together talking and reading Scripture. The mentor spends time in her prayer room, her dedicated War Room, where she goes to battle for her mentee. And because of her fervent prayers, God does some pretty amazing things.

At the end of that movie, I was so moved I couldn't leave.

I stayed in my seat and wept. I loved the mentoring that was portrayed in the movie, and I was inspired by the older woman's passionate (often loud and adoringly animated) prayers, but something bothered me. I kept thinking, what if we had mentors who didn't only go to their prayer rooms alone, but who took the hand of her mentee and tackled war room prayers together? In living rooms, in coffee shops, in church classrooms? What would God do as we connect with each other in such powerful prayer? I believe God would absolutely meet with us and release His power in our world because of our bold, united prayers.

> "*God, raise up the mentors who pray! Pour out a spirit of prayer across our land and do it through prayer-focused mentoring relationships!*"

My prayer because of that movie has become "God, raise up the mentors who pray! Pour out a spirit of prayer across our land and do it through prayer-focused mentoring relationships!"

The world needs us. I understand Christian women wanting to spend time together. That is sweet time. The challenge for each of us is to reach out to those outside our comfort zones to fulfill the great commission as we talked about in Chapter 5. To "go and make disciples" will require us to move beyond our familiar circles. I'm talking to myself here, too. I can become comfortable just like the next person. It's so easy to become complacent within our own preferences and traditions, and when that happens we get stuck.

And tragically, when we're stuck, we don't see change. We aren't experiencing movement or transformation. God may seem silent. The answers to prayer are slow in coming.

I hear those words a lot from those I've mentored, and quite honestly, I've been there myself.

The enemy of our souls doesn't want us to move beyond our past, or even move past our present as long as we're being unproductive for God's Kingdom. He likes it when we're stuck and silent. In contrast, Jesus, the lover of our souls, desires for us to move beyond surviving to thriving, from fear to faith, from worry to worship, from loneliness to togetherness. He wants us walking in freedom and living out an abundant, fruitful life. Jesus desires that for mentors and mentees alike. And guess what?

I believe mentoring is part of His grand plan!

In the past, revivals often happened as organized events on a big stage. Most of us remember watching throngs of new believers fill the aisles to the tune of "Just as I Am" during televised Billy Graham crusades. What I loved most about Billy Graham crusades was the pre-revival praying that happened in cities months before the great evangelist's arrival. God was doing the work through the obedience of Billy Graham and his staff and countless praying volunteers. That's how God wants to use each of us today—through obedience and prayer.

The world around us is changing. Revivals aren't broadcast on national TV very much these days. What if . . . *now stay with me here* . . . what if the next great revival comes through one-on-one, prayer-focused mentoring? Can you see it? With such a desperation for connection and a tireless pursuit of truth among younger generations today who desire more in their lives, mentoring provides the perfect platform to spark a revival. I have friends who have prayed for revival for years and years. Could revival happen through one changed heart at a time? Absolutely!

> *"Could revival happen through one changed heart at a time? Absolutely!"*

As we, the mentors, surrender our desires and draw closer to Jesus, spending diligent time with Him on our own, we will begin to experience a refreshing in our own lives. The definition of refresh is to give new strength or energy to; reinvigorate; revive; breathe new life into. Doesn't that sound wonderful? One of God's promises heralds this truth: *Come near to God and he will come near to you* (James 4:8). That's an undeniable promise we can hang our hat on.

Here's another way of thinking about that verse: If we come near to someone who is full of God, then we will come near to God as well.

The older I get, the more I realize that in every season of my life, it is important to *have* a mentor as well as *be* a mentor. When I've drawn near to my mentor, Fern Nichols, I have drawn near to God. Her joy and peace splashes over on me and I am more joyful and peaceful. Her faith and trust in God overflow into my life so that I want to be more full of faith and trust. When she doesn't sound worried or scared, then I don't feel that either. That's the blessing of having a godly mentor! Sometimes we need an example, someone to model this for us. That's exactly what we do for our mentees.

We show our mentees what it looks like to move beyond our ordinary selves, to have an intimate relationship with Jesus, to be filled with His Spirit, and to walk with God. We do that through the Holy Spirit working within us and extending beyond us.

> *"I love that God chooses ordinary people to do extraordinary things."*

I love that God chooses ordinary people to do extraordinary things. He's looking for humility, dependency, and a posture of availability. We don't need to be dynamic evangelists like Billy Graham; we just need to be ourselves, obedient and willing, longing for more, and letting God do His work through us.

Each of us does our part, leading others closer to Jesus, one person at a time. We pray, fervently and passionately, with our mentees. We ask God to ignite His presence within them, meeting their needs for a life-saving, life-giving relationship. We show them the way to a personal, prayer relationship with Jesus that changes their lives and the lives of those around them. What a magnificent vision! This is a dream I believe God has placed in my heart—one-on-one, prayer-focused mentoring can change the world. You and I can be a part of an extraordinary movement of God. Together, let us dream big!

Will you pray with me?

Lord Jesus, breathe new life into us as mentors. Give us refreshed strength and energy to move beyond our comfort zones, beyond our own limitations, to follow You. Revive us, dear Lord, and have Your way in our lives. Fill us with Your Spirit so we are able to do our part to help others know You. We pray for a revival throughout the land that only You can bring. Amen.

CHAPTER 11

Real Transformation

The most satisfying words I've ever heard a mentee say are, "This has changed my life," and, "This has changed the way I pray." That makes my heart sing! If you ask me why I mentor and why I feel such a passion to share MORE Mentoring with as many people as possible, it's because I've seen a transformed life—and that's worth it all.

Jeannine's story is an example. It took her two years to ask for a mentor. Insecurity had been building a brick wall around her since she was a child. She thought, *Why in the world would I drag someone into my marriage challenges, exhaustion from raising small children—and can I offer anything in return?*

She finally gathered enough courage to ask someone to mentor her, and in her words, "My life has not been the same since that day. I have someone speaking consistent truth over me, my marriage, and my children."

Jeannine's story of transformation can inspire us all. Through her mentoring relationship, the wall of protection started to slowly crumble. Being vulnerable and authentic brought on extreme healing.

Jeannine shares, "I no longer am afraid to share my story and to ask for what I need. My children, marriage, and other relationships are benefiting greatly from these powerful changes. My mentor's friendship, love, and prayers have rebuilt a new kind of wall: a spiritual shield which allows for a much healthier perspective on life, relationships, and mothering. I am loved, accepted, and cared for by God and my mentor no matter what my past experiences have been like, and especially during a stage of motherhood that can feel very lonely. God is good."

"As we keep on pointing our mentees to Jesus, we help set them free—from unforgiveness, from hopelessness, from lies of the enemy."

Our mentees just might come to us with mixed-up mindsets. As we keep on pointing our mentees to Jesus, we help set them free—from unforgiveness, from hopelessness, from lies of the enemy.

Satan is real. He's an accuser and a deceiver. He's a destroyer. He is the king of the "de" words: words that bring death to someone's spirit. He strives to take away. Steal. Tear down.

These are his kind of words:

- Destroy
- Deflate
- Deceive
- Defeat
- Degrade
- Deplete

- Depression
- Despair
- Desperate
- Decline
- Defiance
- Delay

- Deprive
- Destitute
- Devalue
- Devastate

Jesus, on the glorious other hand, is the King of the "re" words—words that breathe life into our spirit. He loves to pour into. Build up. Give back. Keep us moving.

These are His lifegiving kind of words:

- Renew
- Refresh
- Redeem
- Restore
- Rebuild
- Revive

- Reclaim
- Reconcile
- Refuel
- Reignite
- Refine
- Repair

- Repossess
- Re-establish
- Retrieve
- Reward

He is a breakthrough God, a transforming God. There is not one "de" word in your life, or in the life of your mentee, that is too impossible for Him to change into a "re" word. Your very life can be a great display of His power and glory as you welcome His transformation into your life.

A key factor to transformation is the renewing of our minds through the power of God's written Word. We must be aware and alert and not give Satan an opportunity or one little fingernail hold on our lives. So much of the battle happens in our minds. One of the greatest roles a mentor can have is to help a mentee expose the lies, trample them, and then replace them with truth. We must read, study, learn the truth in God's Word, and plant our feet upon it. The more we know the truth, the more we can easily decipher the lies.

> "A key factor to transformation is the renewing of our minds through the power of God's written Word."

Another way to renew our minds and defeat the enemy is through prayer—out loud, in agreement, praising, confessing, thanking, and asking. Praying together is powerful warfare. Besides the obvious aspect of God hearing and answering our prayers, praying together teaches our mentees how to pray when we're not around. And praying alone is essential. We each need that private time alone with Jesus, uninfluenced and uninterrupted by others. We model praying with our mentees so they learn how to talk with Jesus on their own, and eventually become mentors themselves.

Just like a parent raises a child to be independent, a mentor invests in the life of a mentee to see her transformed and independent. We already know we don't carry the pressure on our shoulders to do the transforming. We just invite God into our relationship, and He does the transforming. And here's the exciting benefit—transformation happens in the mentor as well as the mentee!

If we mentor long enough and often enough, transformation is bound to happen in our own lives as well as in our mentees. How could it not? We give, we learn, we pray. Those are actions that will yield a harvest.

Let us not become weary in doing good, for at the proper time we will reap a harvest if we do not give up (Galatians 6:9).

There are times when transformation happens immediately. For example, when someone bows her knee and surrenders her life to Christ, she stands up as a brand-new person. The transformation is real. The old is gone and the new has come. The transformed individual forges ahead with youthful zeal, filled with fresh faith and an insatiable desire to learn more of God's truths.

But oftentimes transformation comes in such small steps, in hardly recognizable, miniscule ways . . . until one day our mentee crosses a persistent

> "*Mentoring really does start in our minds and how we think.*"

hurdle with surprising peace, or we find ourselves booming with unrelenting confidence. Then we know, we know! God is transforming us, making us more like Jesus, just as He promised.

We find ourselves living with a mentoring mindset, or a mentoring lifestyle. Mentoring really does start in our minds and how we think.

A fellow mentor shared with me how her life has been

transformed since she started mentoring. She admitted how she is more mindful of her personal relationship with God. She prays more diligently to be filled with the Holy Spirit so He flows through her to her mentee. She reads her Bible more fervently, scoping out truths to share. She's more mindful of her everyday thoughts and actions as she thinks about her role as a mentor. That in and of itself is a sign of growth, of transformation. We don't only pray and read the Bible with our mentees; we increase that activity in our own life. We live a life of prayer. A life of renewing our minds. A life of growing closer to Jesus. A life of transformation.

A mentoring mindset reflects a sense of responsibility that comes with being a mentor. Not a responsibility to change the mentee, but to draw closer to God ourselves so we can be the mentor our mentee needs. This doesn't mean we just think like a mentor, it means we live like a mentor. We *are* mentors!

Join me in reading the Mentor's Declaration and sense the transforming power of God filling you with each promise.

A Mentor's Declaration

I am a mentor.

I have what it takes and everything I need.

I have Jesus.

His power is at work within me.

I have a purpose and a high calling to invest in people.

My story matters and I will share it to proclaim God's greatness.

I will choose to love, listen, encourage, and pray.

My faith is what pleases God.

My life will have a ripple-effect investment.

I will pour myself out so God can pour Himself in.

I believe in the power of connection—both with God and others.

I was made to be real.

I am qualified through Christ's sufficiency in me.

I am enough because Jesus is enough in me.

I can do all things through Christ who strengthens me.

Talk about a mentoring mindset!

My friend Karen Zummo had a mentoring mindset. She was always looking for and pursuing people who needed a word of encouragement, hope, or truth spoken over them. Her heart was moved with compassion for people and she couldn't help herself. She leaned in and she loved well. To be sure, Karen's story was far from perfect. She walked through some really hard things, but here's the key: she allowed God to use her story for His glory. Even though she is now in heaven, her mentoring mindset will have an impact for years to come.

I look forward to the first time you hear those invaluable five words from your mentee: "This has changed my life." I believe each mentor will be able to say the same thing. From hopelessness to hope, from fearful to full of faith, we move into the fullness of the transformed life God has for us.

CHAPTER 12

Real Multiplication

Taryn became a mother at the age of 16. During those difficult times, she had mentors who poured into her life. Her mom supported her with encouragement, and others from her church listened to her, challenged her, and sowed into this teen mom a love of prayer, Scripture, and awareness of the Holy Spirit. Each of those mentors saw the story of a young woman just beginning. They couldn't have realized at the time how much their efforts would be multiplied.

In her new role as a mom, Taryn felt exhausted, not only with the care of a newborn, but also with the tension between believing God had a purpose for her life and the contrasting heavy burden of loneliness, depression, and lack of confidence. A prominent message kept running through her head, *You're too young.* But one thing remained constant—her mentors never gave up meeting with her.

Eventually, the lie of being *too young to be useful* dimmed. And not just because she got older. Exposing the lie and speaking it aloud to someone older and wiser diminished its paralyzing grip. And when the distraction was gone, it opened space for Taryn's purpose to be illuminated—to mentor other women who saw no glimpse of hope. Through her tough experiences, Taryn obtained immense empathy. She gained the ability to understand and personally share the same feelings of others who had gone through all she had.

Taryn shares her story:

"That strenuous season of pregnancy and young motherhood felt void of purpose for me. What I couldn't notice then was that I was developing a dependence on God. After all, how was I supposed to connect to deep pain if God hadn't allowed that dark period in my life? He opened my eyes to the awareness that I wasn't the only one experiencing painful loneliness. In fact, when I lifted my eyes off myself, I could not only empathize with so many other hurting women, but I could also see that the lack of community was immense, especially for young, single moms.

> *He opened my eyes to the awareness that I wasn't the only one experiencing painful loneliness.*

"One night, a mentor urged me to start a mom's group for women in a similar situation. It was confirmation of a thought I'd had 100 times over. From that extra spark of encouragement,

I took steps of boldness and said 'yes' to whatever God had ahead. What started as building community for myself transformed into a local ministry for young moms who didn't feel like they fit in anywhere else.

"The lie of being too young sat deeply as I began the journey of ministry building. And I believed it. Deafeningly so when it came to mentoring other moms. But for every voice that uttered that statement over my calling, there were three louder ones speaking life from the front row. Graciously, God put people in my life who poured lavishly into me. My mentors emboldened me to gather other women in my life and invest generously—invest in their stories and giftings, listen to their desires and hurts and everything in between. Now, several years later, I'm praying about starting my own business and coaching women, which really just looks like mentoring in a lot of ways."

Taryn now mentors women into boldness through the Holy Spirit's leading, and recently became a trained Christian coach. The multiplication continues!

It's been a long time since I've felt too young to be useful. Still, last week I had one of *those* weeks. You know the kind. I was crazy busy, doing a lot and not seeing much progress, and I began to think, "Does any of this make a difference?" Do you ever feel that way? Your wheels are spinning, your to-do list is long, and you stop to gain perspective—will any of this really matter for eternity?

Then, I received two phone calls in one day. Both calls were from mentees who told me about their courage to step out in faith and become mentors themselves.

The Lord encouraged my heart by whispering in my ear, "This is the ripple effect your life is making, Nancy."

"But I'm just one drop in an ocean of many drops."

"Yes, but you are one significant drop."

And just like me, you are a very important drop as well.

At MORE Mentoring, we talk a lot about pouring into others. Our main image for our ministry shows a pitcher of water pouring out into another container. There is so much significance to that choice of design. As mentors, we allow the Holy Spirit to fill us with His presence, like cool, refreshing water into our souls. From that fullness, we pour into the lives of our mentees.

> "A ripple begins with one drop of water. It can seem small and insignificant. But the ripples that circle out from that one drop create more drops that in turn create more drops."

If you look closely at the picture of pouring water, you'll notice one of my favorite parts. The water pouring from the pitcher is creating a series of ripples. If we could use a moving graphic, I'd choose to show those ripples expanding to the edge of the cup, overflowing into another bigger container, and then keep on rippling into bigger and bigger containers as far as the eye can see, like an eternal, layered water fountain. That's the picture I have in my mind of how mentoring multiplies. It's the *ripple-effect investment.*

A ripple begins with one drop of water. It can seem small and insignificant. But the ripples that circle out from that one drop create more drops that in turn create more drops. Mentors don't want to pour in and have the flow stop at the rim. Unfortunately, this can happen.

Some mentor/mentee relationships blossom into such great friendships that neither one wants to move on to other mentoring relationships. I say, "Be a mentor for a season and a friend for life." You can still be friends, but don't get stuck in a comfortable trap. Other relationships may not end so well. If you are working with a mentee who is dealing with some heavier issues that may require professional help or she doesn't mature or want to move on, things can get sticky. But don't let those rare times discourage you from pouring into other new mentees. There are new ripples to be made.

One drop can have a ripple effect that makes a great impact when it expands far and wide. Imagine a ripple-effect investment in mentoring that flows across the globe!

Here's what it looks like. We ask our mentee questions, listen to her concerns, share our story, and lead her to some of our favorite Scriptures. We come alongside her for a season, pouring God's love into her until she's ready to move on. The pouring might just simply be speaking a word of encouragement, or sharing a verse, or whispering truth in someone's ear. It doesn't have to be a full-blown sermon. *Thank you, Jesus!*

Then the baton gets passed. We find someone new to mentor and our mentee becomes a mentor, with a new mentee of her own. These new mentors pour into new mentees, and *their* mentees connect with others, and on and on it goes. Changed lives change lives.

We invest in one person, but that person might invest
"Changed lives change lives." in 30 people. I've personally watched this play out in my life. Sarah's story in the beginning of this book is a perfect example. She was the first one to ask me to be a mentor. I simply poured in. And then I watched God use Sarah to impact so many other peoples' lives. I saw the ripple-effect investment taking place before my very eyes.

We often think we are giving so little that what we're doing won't really matter. But it does. God's promise of "I will bless you. I will multiply you," rings in my ears often. God's promise frees me from thinking I have to multiply myself or this ministry that He's called me to lead. Although mentoring is not happening widely across the church yet, I can see the ripple effect of transformed mentors and mentees reaching out to their pastors and women's ministry leaders, saying "We need this!" Women telling women how mentoring changed their lives is powerful.

God keeps reminding me that real greatness is in the quiet, behind-the-scenes pouring into others' lives. It's one by one by one. Here at MORE Mentoring, we care about the *one*. The one who is lonely or feels disconnected and isolated. The one who is overwhelmed with life and just needs to hear some words of hope. The one who might be fearful, anxious, or worried and needs to hear "I've been there." The one who is ripe and ready and eager for a mentor who is just a little bit further ahead on her spiritual journey.

I'm not called to preach to the masses. Most of us aren't. But we are called to care for the one.

The day before my deadline for finishing the first draft of this book, I had a mentoring appointment scheduled. I could have easily rescheduled to make sure I got this done but the Lord planted this thought in my mind, *This mentoring relationship is what this book is all about. If you don't take time to mentor, the book will mean nothing.* My life wouldn't be living out what I'm writing about.

So I went off with joy and met with my mentee for our hour-and-a-half, and it was such a confirmation of experiencing "Mentoring Made Real." I love how God speaks to us in such personal ways. I surrendered my deadline to God, just like we surrender our mentoring relationships to Him.

Here's my encouragement to you today: Be the drop that makes a ripple effect. Care about the one. Watch God multiply that small investment and bless it beyond anything you could imagine. Yes, we are each one bitty drop, but together we are creating a movement that can change the church and the world.

CONCLUSION

Taking Action

Mentoring made real. Real people, real needs, real connections, real results. I hope that by reading these stories of real mentors and real mentees in real life situations, you are ready to take real action!

The very core of MORE Mentoring is connecting with the heart of God through our supportive relationships and especially through our prayers. That's why I love prayer-focused mentoring so much! We enter into prayer with our mentees, surrendering all to Jesus, seeking Him for guidance, waiting for His answers. And as we do, the Holy Spirit fills us with His life-giving power. His power transforms and heals. He revitalizes our lives—both mentor and mentee.

I long for women (and men) around the world to experience more of Jesus, His fullness of life, the fruitfulness that comes from a life of freedom, joy, peace, and hope. Do I think that's attainable? Yes, I do!

Like I said earlier, I have such a great passion for mentoring because I have seen God transform lives through it. Mentoring is all about relationships—growing in our relationship with God and with others. I believe one-on-one mentoring could cause a shift in our culture and diminish the disconnection we all feel, and it would strengthen our marriages, families, neighborhoods, and churches.

At MORE Mentoring, we long to see mentors rise up and show up. Mentors show up *real* rather than having all the best advice or the perfect answers. They just love, listen, encourage, and pray. As you've seen, it doesn't have to be complicated.

When prayer is the foundation of our mentoring relationships, it takes all the pressure and weight off the mentor's shoulders and transfers it to God's shoulders. Prayer changes our mentoring from the natural to the supernatural. It's not our wisdom, but God's.

My prayer is that God will pour out a spirit of prayer and expand a mentoring movement across our land, and that it will multiply within the Church—those of us who know our God and can share His love with others in real and life-giving ways, even potentially life-saving ways.

During the time my husband and I lived in Denver, a desperate young mom who lived not far from our house reached a devastating breaking point. One bleak day, she killed her two boys and then took her own life. When I heard the tragic news,

I couldn't help thinking:

What if she'd had a mentor? Someone who really knew her. Someone she could talk with about her desperation. A mentor in her life could have potentially saved her life and the lives of her children. Only God knows.

There is something undeniably powerful that happens when a mentor is present in another person's life.

What if every mom had a mentor encouraging her with words of hope?

What if every middle school and high school student had a spiritual mentor?

What if every lonely person had someone care about him or her?

It would absolutely change the world.

As you have read the stories throughout this book of how people's lives have been changed and greatly benefited from prayer-focused mentoring, my prayer is that your heart is stirred to take the first step.

Three simple steps can get you on your way to a mentoring relationship.

Pray, Pursue, Participate

First of all, **pray.** Ask God who it is that He might want you to form a mentoring relationship with, who He wants you to invest in. Ask Him for strength and wisdom and discernment to know what to say and how to say it. Be honest and real with Him. He knows your heart better than you do. He will guide you. Be watching for someone you could invest in and also someone who could invest in you. It might be someone you aren't even thinking about. Maybe it's a neighbor or a co-worker or a relative or someone at church. When God leads you, it will be a divine and glorious connection. Begin praying for her as soon as you know who she is. In fact, you could start praying for her now!

Next, **pursue**. Nothing will happen unless somebody takes the first step. Be intentional. Be invitational. Be bold. Be fearless. Maybe it's simply asking, "Do you want to grab coffee? I would love to hear your story." Get involved at your church. That's a great place to look for a mentor or a mentee.

Finally, **participate**. Be involved. Get in the front seat, lean in, learn all you can. You can trust God with the outcome. It's a whole lot more fun and adventurous to take a risky step forward that way. You do your part. Let God do His part. Simply walk alongside someone and point her to Jesus.

That's it. Pray. Pursue. Participate.

Pray for that person God has for you to mentor.

Pursue that relationship—knowing God has prepared her heart.

Participate in God's plan of redemption and growth.

I have prayed for each reader while I was writing this book. If you've stayed with me this far to the end of the book,

I believe you are chosen and anointed to have a life-changing effect on someone else's life. Will you join me in this mentoring movement? Will you be the one to care about the *one*? Who is your *one*? There's no better time to start mentoring than today. Let's do this together.

IF YOU WANT
MORE

CONNECTION QUESTIONS

Introduction

1. Share about a time in your life when you didn't feel seen, heard, or known.

2. Do you currently have a mentor?

3. Are you currently mentoring someone else?

4. Who is someone in your life who has been a natural mentor to you (with or without the formal title)?

5. What qualities do you love about that person?

Part 1 - Come

1. Is mentoring important to you (why/why not)?

2. What does it mean to you to come alongside another person?

3. What are the real needs that you see in your circle of influence?

4. What concerns do you have either as a mentor or a mentee?

5. What new idea stands out to you in understanding generational differences?

Part 2 - Be

1. What is unique about your story or experiences that could bring value to your mentee/mentor?

2. What are the challenges/benefits that come with pursuing someone of a different ethnicity or culture?

3. Which of the 4 Pillars of Mentoring (Love, Listen, Encourage, Pray) are the hardest/easiest for you?

4. Does prayer-focused mentoring make you feel relieved or fearful? Why?

5. Have you ever trusted in another person or God and been let down? Share the experience and the feelings that came with it.

Part 3 - Move

1. After reading that a mentor doesn't have to be perfect but present, can you see yourself in that role?

2. What is your next step of action in moving towards a mentoring relationship (Pray, Pursue, Participate)?

3. What kind of transformation do you long to experience or have you experienced as a result of being in a mentoring relationship?

4. Share about a time when you saw the ripple-effect investment take place in another person's life.

5. Can you see yourself becoming a mentor? Explain.

Conclusion

1. What is holding you back from taking action?

2. As you pray, who is it that God is putting on your
    heart to ask to be a mentor/mentee?

3. Who will you pursue and how will you pursue her?

4. How can you participate in another person's life?
    Write down some specific goals and see how God
    comes through as you step out in faith.

5. What next action step will you take (rising up as a
    mentor, asking someone to be your mentor, sharing
    the need with your church, taking the mentoring
    mindset to your community or organization)?

Knowing the Greatest Mentor

When you think of the greatest mentor of all time, who do you think of? I can think of certain people in my life I have come to know personally. They haven't been the people on a stage or someone far off who I just admire. They have been those people who see me, hear me, and know me. They have been the ones I have connected with heart to heart. I have had some really great mentors in my life, but none come even close to comparing to God. He is actually three mentors wrapped up into one—God the Father, God the Son, and God the Holy Spirit.

Do you know Him? Not just about Him, but *really know* Him?

When you really know Him, you understand that He is always with you. He speaks to you. He defends you. He comforts you. He has all the answers to your problems. He accepts you. He gives you perfect peace that you can't even understand. He loves you unconditionally. He has time for you. He is patient with you. He is kind. He is full of grace. He wants to answer your prayers in miraculous ways. He knows your future. He protects you. He frees you from fear and anxiety. He is forgiving. He is for you. He sees you. He hears you. He knows you.

Every earthly mentor will fall short of this great Mentor. We can't expect human mentors to meet our every need—only God can do that. He wants to satisfy the longings in your heart.

Do you want a relationship with Him? He wants one with you.

You can simply . . .

1. **Invite Him in.** Open up your heart and life to Him. Be sorry for the sin that separates you from Him. Let Him know that you want Him and that you need Him. Believe that He loves you and accepts you.

2. **Receive His gifts.** Once you invite Him in, He will give you gifts. He gave the greatest gift of all—His Son Jesus, who came to earth to die for you and rose again so that you can have eternal life. He also gives the Holy Spirit to come and live within you and never leave you. He gives spiritual gifts, new clothes, a new name, and fullness of life. What amazing gifts He has to offer if we will just receive them.

3. **Commune with Him.** Talk with Him. He wants to talk with you. That's what prayer is—a beautiful, authentic connection with God that includes both listening and speaking. He has given you His Word, the Bible. Ask Him to speak to you as you read it. Find a community of other believers—maybe that's a church or a mentor. You will find yourself communing with Him as you commune with others who know Him.

God is real. Heaven is real. Hell is real. Eternity is real.

It's only in having a relationship with God that you can know you will spend eternity with Him in heaven. I want you there. He wants you there.

Do you want to be there? If so, you can pray this simple prayer:

God, I want a relationship with You. I invite You into my life. I believe that You love me and that You sent Your Son Jesus to die for me. I'm sorry for my sins that have separated us. I receive the gifts You have to offer me. I desire to know You and to commune with You. Bring people into my life who can help me know what it means to have a relationship with You. In Jesus' name, amen.

1. Invite Him in.

Isaiah 59:1-2, John 3:16, John 17:3, Romans 3:23, Romans 10:9-10

2. Receive His gifts.

Isaiah 61:10, Isaiah 62:2, John 14:16-17, Romans 6:23

3. Commune with Him.

John 15:1-17, John 16:13, John 17:15-25

Scriptures on Mentoring

And let us not give up meeting together. Some are in the habit of doing this. Instead, let us encourage one another with words of hope. Let us do this even more as you see Christ's return approaching (Hebrews 10:25, NIRV).

Two are better than one, because they have a good return for their labor: If either of them falls down, one can help the other up. But pity anyone who falls and has no one to help them up (Ecclesiastes 4:9-10).

Everyone should be quick to listen, slow to speak and slow to become angry (James 1:19b).

Therefore consider carefully how you listen (Luke 8:18a).

Let the wise listen and add to their learning (Proverbs 1:5a).

To answer before listening—that is folly and shame (Proverbs 18:13).

Glorify the LORD with me; let us exalt his name together (Psalm 34:3).

Again, truly I tell you that if two of you on earth agree about anything they ask for, it will be done for them by my Father in heaven. For where two or three gather in my name, there am I with them (Matthew 18:19-20).

Therefore confess your sins to each other and pray for each other so that you may be healed. The prayer of a righteous person is powerful and effective (James 5:16).

I keep asking that the God of our Lord Jesus Christ, the glorious Father, may give you the Spirit of wisdom and revelation, so that you may know him better. I pray that the eyes of your heart may be enlightened in order that you may know the hope to which he has called you, the riches of his glorious inheritance in his holy people (Ephesians 1:17-18).

Whoever refreshes others will be refreshed (Proverbs 11:25b).

Come near to God and he will come near to you (James 4:8a).

Follow my example, as I follow the example of Christ (1 Corinthians 11:1).

And to know this love that surpasses knowledge—that you may be filled to the measure of all the fullness of God. Now to him who is able to do immeasurably more than all we ask or imagine, according to his power that is at work within us, to him be glory in the church and in Christ Jesus throughout all generations, for ever and ever! Amen (Ephesians 3:19-21).

I came that they may have and enjoy life, and have it in abundance [to the full, till it overflows] (John 10:10b, AMP).

He must increase, but I must decrease (John 3:30, ESV).

His divine power has given us everything we need for a godly life through our knowledge of him who called us by his own glory and goodness (2 Peter 1:3).

May the God of hope fill you with all joy and peace as you trust in him, so that you may overflow with hope by the power of the Holy Spirit (Romans 15:13).

Praise be to the Lord, to God our Savior, who daily bears our burdens (Psalm 68:19).

Carry each other's burdens, and in this way you will fulfill the law of Christ (Galatians 6:2).

Not that we are sufficiently qualified in ourselves to claim anything as coming from us, but our sufficiency and qualifications come from God. He has qualified us [making us sufficient] (2 Corinthians 3:5-6a, AMP).

As iron sharpens iron, so one person sharpens another (Proverbs 27:17).

When she speaks she has something worthwhile to say, and she always says it kindly (Proverbs 31:26, MSG).

MORE Mentoring Resources

At MORE Mentoring (*morementoring.org*), we desire to equip and empower you in your mentoring relationships. We want to see you develop and grow, so we offer a toolkit consisting of four components.

Together Toolkit

1. Mentoring guides—books for mentors and mentees to go through together that give ideas for conversation starters, encouragement starters, and prayer starters.

2. Mentor training course—a series of videos to guide mentors as they are starting out.

3. Ministry development course—a series of videos to guide a mentoring leadership team at a church or organization, helping you connect mentors and mentees by giving you some structure and a process to walk through together.

4. A community—women who will help answer questions, share their stories, and encourage each other in the mentoring process.

Message to Churches

Benefits for a Church Mentoring Ministry

My personal passion and the core of who we are at MORE Mentoring is to come alongside local churches and equip them in helping mentoring become a priority. Here are some of the benefits that your church will experience as we help you along the way.

Your Church Will Significantly Benefit From MORE Mentoring.

Here's how . . .

1

We'll PROTECT your time.

If you are like most churches, your staff is busy. Everyone's plate is already full—there's really no margin to take on new things. We understand that. That's why MORE Mentoring provides simple, easy tools designed specifically for equipping lay leaders, people in your church body, to be the catalysts of a mentoring movement in your church. We're here to equip men and women who are available, excited, ready, and willing to make mentoring an integral part of your church community.

2

We provide a PLAN.

MORE Mentoring has already done all the heavy lifting for launching or enriching a mentoring movement in your church. We have a time-tested plan—carefully designed tools and resources that offer you a sturdy framework but also a lot of freedom to fit the culture of your church community.

3

We PREPARE your people.

MORE Mentoring equips mentors by reminding them they have everything they need in Jesus. We help remove the fear and feelings of being unqualified by defining a mentor as someone with a little more experience who comes alongside another and points him or her to Jesus. We keep it simple, yet powerful: Love. Listen. Encourage. Pray.

4

We prioritize PRAYER.

MORE Mentoring is prayer-focused because we know that God unifies and transforms people through prayer. We believe that by encouraging and teaching others to pray together, your entire church family benefits. Prayer becomes a priority and an expected part of relationships and conversations. From these transformed relationships, your people will begin to reach your community and beyond.

Acknowledgements

I'm so grateful for each person who has had a part in helping with the writing of this book! There are many of you who have prayed so faithfully and I know that has made all the difference. A special thanks to Diane Glass, Jill Reding, Sandy Benson, Kim Churness, Anne Neubauer, and the whole MORE Mentoring team. You have consistently gone to the Throne Room on my behalf and I'm eternally grateful.

A big thank you goes to Kathy Groom, Betsy Zenz, Carol Madison, Faith Lefever, Stacey Roszhart, and Sophie Danielson for your beautiful editing touches and graphic design throughout this book. I couldn't have written this without your expertise and creativity. I so appreciate your willingness to step in and help get this book to the finish line.

My wonderful family has been so supportive and encouraging. A special thanks to my parents, Herb and Ardys Roszhart, and to my in-laws, Clayton and Emmy Lou Lindgren. You have been my mentors from the beginning and have modeled so beautifully what it looks like to walk with Jesus on a day-to-day basis. Thanks for faithfully pointing me to Him.

Mark, you are my rock and steady companion. I love how God has made you so different from me. I continue to be mentored by you. Thanks for putting up with an unruly mentee at times!

For those of you stepping into mentoring relationships, your stories of transformation keep me going and are such a great encouragement to my heart. Keep sharing what God is doing in your life through prayer-focused mentoring. You are making a ripple-effect investment that will impact eternity!

God, I will forever be in awe of You. You are the love of my life and will always be my Greatest Mentor. I'm amazed by the transforming work You continue to do in my life and many lives around me. All praise, glory, and honor goes to You for anything good that may come from this book.